Nearly Everything
About
Chinese Characters

汉字的现代基本知识

WU Gaofeng

Illustrations by WU Longwei

SC
Sky Connection

Nearly Everything About Chinese Characters
汉字的现代基本知识

Published in Great Britain by
Sky Connection Ltd,
3 Steeple Walk, Reading, Berkshire RG6 4HR

Copyright © Wu Gaofeng 2008
Illustrations by Wu Longwei

British Library Cataloguing in Publication Data
Data available

ISBN 978-0-9559354-0-4

1 3 5 7 9 10 8 6 4 2

Printed and bound in Great Britain by
Biddles Ltd, King's Lynn, Norfolk

To my parents, *Wu Longwei* and *Cheng Shulian*

To *Bing* and *Shan*

About the Author
作者简介

Wu Gaofeng's career straddles academia, engineering and information technology.

He was born in China, and was awarded BSc (1982), MSc (1985) and PhD (1989) in Engineering from *Dalian* University of Technology. He, with his wife and daughter, came to the UK at the beginning of the 1990s, and now lives in Berkshire, England.

He started to teach his daughter reading and writing Chinese at home when she was 8. The teaching experience was immensely challenging and enjoyable. This book is based on his 7 years teaching and 4 years research and writing.

This is his first book.

Acknowledgements
致谢

This book would not have been possible without the enormous existing resources open to me digitally on the Internet and conventionally on paper. A Chinese proverb that originated from Confucius says: "I hear and I forget; I see and I remember; I do and I understand." I have benefited and learnt a great deal during the course of completing the book. I am truly grateful and indebted to all the related works — read and studied directly or indirectly.

This work is a synergistic product of my family, the idea for which was conceived after I started to teach my daughter *Shan* Chinese at home when she was 8 years old. My father *Wu Longwei* has not only penned all the calligraphy work in the book but also provided me with his ideas and proposals at the beginning of the project. I am so proud to have a wonderful and smart daughter like *Shan*. For the last few years, she has been like my English tutor and has helped me immensely with my endless questions with regard to writing in English and English grammar. My profoundest thanks go to my incomparable and patient wife, *Qu Bing*, for her encouragement and support during the course of the project. Her intuition and constructive criticism allowed me to make the book be a much better and easier read than it would have been otherwise.

Drafts have been read by Cathy McLennan, to whom I am deeply grateful for her shrewd suggestions.

To all the volunteers and friends who responded to my survey questionnaire about the 'basic and elementary' Chinese characters, I appreciate the collaboration and help.

Contents

目录

Writing is among the greatest inventions in human history, perhaps the greatest invention, since it made history possible.
　　　Andrew Robinson (***The Story of Writing***)

A different language is a different vision of life.
　　　Federico Fellini

It is one thing to use language; it is quite another to understand how it works.
　　　Anthony Burgess (***Joysprick***)

Introduction
引言

This book is about Chinese characters, which are referred to as *hanzi* — 汉字 in China.

It introduces the beauty, wonder and appreciation of Chinese characters at a level that is neither too demanding nor lacking depth, but is fun and balanced in its coverage of a fascinating subject.

Stories behind the Book

As someone who grew up and was educated in China, I had always taken the Chinese language and writing system for granted, and had never realized that I was actually quite ignorant of many aspects of my native language until I was asked some basic 'what', 'why' and 'how' questions by non-Chinese speakers. When I decided to start teaching my daughter Chinese myself at home when she was 8 years old, I did not know what a long and challenging journey I would be undertaking.

My daughter arrived in Britain when she was two and a half years old. Since then, she has been living in a bilingual environment: Chinese at home and with relatives in China during the summer holidays, and English at school and with her friends. Because of this, her speaking and listening to Chinese has never been a problem. For her, the problem with the Chinese language has always been Chinese characters, and reading and writing Chinese. From the moment that I decided to teach her Chinese at home, I started to search and prepare all the relevant materials needed to be able to answer all her questions, be able to make the lessons fun and interesting, and be able to tell her stories and draw her pictures. That was when the idea of writing a book like this started.

In 1997 I joined a multi-national IT company, who specializes in providing banking applications to banks and financial institutions in more than 120 countries. Being exposed to languages other than English never seems special to my colleagues, but they are always fascinated by Chinese characters. From time to time, they would ask me to write the Chinese equivalents of English words such as love — 爱, angel — 天使, football — 足球 etc. It might have been to surprise their children or other family members on a card or perhaps just out of curiosity.

On 13th July 2001 at the 112th IOC Session in Moscow, *Beijing* was elected the Host City for the Games of the XXIX Olympiad in 2008. Hosting the Olympics in the world's most populous country for the first time, China, with its thousands of years of civilization and culture, will welcome participants and visitors from all over the world. "When in Rome, do as the Romans do." In the summer of 2008, in *Beijing*, non-Chinese speakers would very much like to be able to speak some basic Chinese, to read and write some simple Chinese characters, and to gain some knowledge about Chinese history and Chinese characters while enjoying the games.

One summer's day in 2002, I accompanied my wife to the Royal Berkshire Hospital in Reading. While sitting in the waiting room, I noticed a couple of Chinese calligraphy works hanging on the wall, so I went over to read those artistic works. What followed was an enjoyable chat with some of the people waiting there. I was deeply impressed by their fondness and appreciation of Chinese characters. To them, Chinese characters are just small, pretty pictures.

A British friend of mine, whose wife is Chinese, once complained to me about the steep learning curve he was experiencing with Chinese characters: "I can handle Chinese sounds. You get used to them, to some degree, when you have been exposed to a Chinese speaking environment for a while. But Chinese characters really give me a headache; I just can't imagine how you can manage a couple of thousand of them. I desperately need some inspiration."

There are more such stories from my personal experiences since I came to Britain, but too many to list here.

A Thousand-Mile Journey Takes Every Step

Inspired by all of the above, I decided that I would devote a portion of my life to reading books and journal articles, to searching the Internet, and to carrying out surveys when necessary while teaching my daughter Chinese at home. The idea was to write a book that would blend the following three objectives: interesting and inspirational jump-start reading; concise but accurate coverage of all the key aspects of *hanzi*; essential and long lasting reference. That was my dream, a long dream indeed. From the day I first drafted the contents and outline, it's been almost 4 years down the road. I never expected it would take this long.

"A thousand-mile journey takes every step," *Xunzi*, a Chinese philosopher who lived during the period of Warring States, said more than 2000 years ago. This book is here to dispel mystique, to help and inspire readers. Most importantly, it will be a companion in readers' journey towards learning and better understanding the Chinese language and *hanzi*.

Welcome and enjoy.

Timeline
时间线

BC	
c. 3400	Sumerian cuneiform
c. 3000	Egyptian hieroglyphics
c. 2500	Indus valley script
c. 1800	Linear A
c. 1600	Phoenician alphabetic script
c. 1400	Linear B
c. 1300	*Yinxu* oracle bone script in China
551 – 479	Confucius
479 – 338	Period of Greek classical culture: Socrates, Plato, Pindar, Herodotus etc.
c. 372 – 289	Mencius
c. 221 – 207	The small seal script of Chinese characters
206	The Great Wall was completed
c. 215 BC – 220 AD	The clerical script of Chinese characters
c. 93 BC	*Sima Qian* completed **Records of the Grand Historian of China**

AD	
c. 105	Invention of paper in China
110	*Xu Shen* compiled the etymological dictionary of Chinese characters: ***Shuowen Jiezi***
c. 271	Magnetic compass in use in China
c. 581 – 907	The regular script of Chinese characters (as used today)
730	Block printing in China
776	Traditional date of the first Olympic Games in Greece
c. 863	Creation of Cyrillic alphabet in eastern Europe
c. 900	Gunpowder in China
1040	Movable type printing was invented in China
1100	First universities in Europe were founded: Salerno, Bologna and Paris
c. 1096 – 1167	University of Oxford was founded
1209	University of Cambridge was founded
1400	Early versions of the novels **Romance of the Three Kingdoms** and **Water Margin** were published
1455	Johannes Gutenberg printed the first book in Europe in movable type

c. 1500	Italian Renaissance: da Vinci, Michelangelo, Raphael, Botticelli etc.
1564 – 1616	William Shakespeare
c. 1610	Scientific revolution in Europe began: Kepler, Bacon, Galileo, Descartes etc.
1636	Harvard University was founded
1687	Isaac Newton's **Principia**
1701	Yale College was founded in the USA
1716	*Kangxi* **Dictionary** was completed with 47035 characters
1768	First edition of the **Encyclopedia Britannica**
1791	*Cao Xueqin*'s novel **A Dream of Red Mansions** was published
1812	The first rotary printing press moved by steam started to work at **The Times** in London
1826	First photographic image was produced in France
1859	Darwin published **The Origin of Species**
1860	Great age of European novels: Dickens, Dumas, Flaubert, Turgenev, Tolstoy etc.
1876	Bell filed his first patent on the telephone
1905	Einstein's **Theory of Relativity**
1928	The first transatlantic television signal, between London and New York, was broadcasted
1948	Transistor and first storage computer were developed
1956	The People's Republic of China (PRC) issued official Chinese character simplification
1958	*Pinyin* was approved in the PRC
1958	The first communications satellite was launched
1963	ASCII was published
1981	MS-DOS was released for PC compatible platform
1983	TCP/IP became the core Internet protocol
1985	Fax machine commercially available
1980s	Spread of personal computers in offices and homes in the western world
1987	**Economic Daily** in China adopted Chinese characters laser phototypesetting system
1989 – 1990	WWW project was launched in 1989, and the first web page appeared in 1990
1991	Unicode 1.0 was published
1990s	Mobile phone culture started to evolve
2000s	SMS is gaining great momentum, and 'texting' is becoming a popular culture

Chinese Characters — *Hanzi*: The Origins and Development

汉字的起源及演变

1

"The most beautiful thing we can experience is the mysterious. It is the source of all true art and all science."
Albert Einstein

"To know the truth of history is to realize its ultimate myth and its inevitable ambiguity."
Roy P. Basler

Chinese characters, commonly known as *hanzi*, are the most fascinating and mysterious writing characters presently in use in the world. Not only have *hanzi* been used by Chinese people to communicate and record information for thousands of years, but the beauty and wonder of *hanzi* are now increasingly attracting interest all over the world. Different from characters used in other languages, *hanzi* are a collection of picturesque and mostly meaningful logograms. Both inside and outside of China, as an art or a hobby, Chinese calligraphy is widely admired and practised.

Today there are two types of *hanzi* in use: Simplified Chinese Characters (SCC) and Complex Chinese Characters (CCC), which are also referred to as Traditional Chinese Characters (TCC). The main differences between these two types of *hanzi* are:
- SCC are broadly used throughout China and Singapore.
- CCC are mainly used in Taiwan, Hong Kong and Macao.
- CCC had been the sole Chinese writing system until SCC were put into use in the People's Republic of China in 1956.[†]
- SCC are the end result of successive undertakings to simplify CCC in China since 1949.[‡]

[†] The People's Republic of China issued its first round of official character simplification in 1956.[1]

[‡] The People's Republic of China was established on 1st October 1949.

1.1 The Origins of *Hanzi*

The origins of things such as the universe, life, languages, writing systems and legends always fascinate, puzzle and inspire us.

The earliest written record on the origins of Chinese characters can be traced back to some 2000 years ago. Since the discovery of oracle bone script in 1899,[†] to understand and reveal the origins of *hanzi* has been the holy grail of the study of the Chinese writing system.

Despite the unearthing of many archaeological sites, the great advance in technology, and enormous research work by scholars and scientists in archaeology, anthropology, history and psychology in the 20th century, many questions regarding the origins of Chinese characters still remain. When and where did writing start to emerge in China? How did it develop into the oracle bone script of the *Shang* dynasty? Here, the pictures blur, the theories differ, and the enigma remains unsolved.

1.1.1 Legends

Until the discovery of oracle bone script, the explanations of the origins of Chinese characters were only available from written records, and they were dominated by myths and legends.

Out of all the legends, the one in which *Cang Jie* created Chinese characters was arguably most popular. As appeared in many literary works [4–7] during the Warring States and in the early etymological dictionary **Shuowen Jiezi**,[‡] the legend has it that *Cang Jie*, who was claimed to be the official historian of the Yellow Emperor, invented Chinese characters in the 27th century BC.

Other explanations include knotted cords and *bagua* (literally 'eight trigrams') — a fundamental philosophical concept in ancient China.

[†] *Wang Yirong* is regarded as the first person who recognized oracle bone script in 1899.[2, 3]

[‡] **Shuowen Jiezi**, literally meaning **Explaining Simple and Analysing Compound Characters**, was compiled by *Xu Shen* between 100AD and 121AD.[8]

1.1.2 Fragmentary yet significant archaeological evidence

Figure 1.1: Six of the archaeological sites within the regions
along the Yellow River and *Yangzi* River.

So far a large number of archaeological sites have been unearthed
in China, most of which were discovered and excavated after 1949.
Although these sites are scattered all over China, a significant
proportion of them are actually located within the regions along the
Yellow River and *Yangzi* River. The six sites shown in Figure 1.1
are some of the archaeological sites which have been found to be
significant in the search for the origins of Chinese characters.

The Six Archeological Sites Shown in Figure 1.1:

1) *Jiahu*

Located in *Wuyang* of *Henan* province, dated *c.* 7000–5800 BC, discovered in 1961, the archaeological site of *Jiahu* is a Neolithic Yellow River settlement of *Peiligang* culture. Artifacts unearthed there include pottery, playable tonal flutes and tortoise shells. Significantly, 20 marks/signs have been discovered, among which two of the 9 incised signs on tortoise shells are very intriguing.[9, 10]

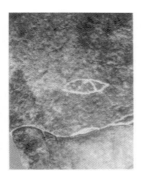

Figure 1.2: Two incised signs on tortoise shells unearthed from the archaeological site of *Jiahu*.

2) *Shuangdun*

Figure 1.3: Signs/symbols found from the carved pottery wares unearthed from the archaeological site of *Shuangdun*.

Located in *Bangbu* of *Anhui* province, dated *c*. 5000 BC, discovered in 1985, the site was excavated from 1986 to 1992. The cultural relics from the site include pottery, various implements made of stone or animal bone, utensils and clay figures. Significantly, over 600 pottery wares have been found bearing carved signs/symbols. These carved pots include mainly bowls and cups, with all the signs/symbols either on the back or on a hidden part of the bowls and cups.[11]

3) *Banpo*

Located by the *Chan* River and some 5 kilometres to the east of *Xi'an* of *Shaanxi* province, dated *c*. 4800–4300 BC, the archaeological site of *Banpo* is a Neolithic village of *Yangshao* culture. Discovered in 1953, the site was excavated in the 1950s by the Chinese Academy of Sciences. Artifacts unearthed from the site include agricultural, hunting and fishing tools, and numerous (painted) pottery vessels and potsherds. Significantly, on those unearthed pottery vessels and potsherds, 30 incised signs/marks have been discovered.[12]

Figure 1.4: 30 incised signs/marks on pottery dated
c. 4800–4300 BC and unearthed from *Banpo*.

4) *Dawenkou*

Located in *Tai'an* of *Shandong* province, dated *c*. 3500–2500 BC, excavated in 1959, the archaeological site of *Dawenkou* is a Neolithic clan cemetery. *Dawenkou* culture is named after the site, which is characterized by the emergence of delicate wheel-made pots of various colours. Significantly, several character-like symbols have been found incised on the unearthed pottery wares belonging to *Dawenkou* culture.

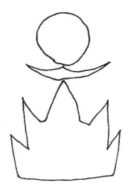

Figure 1.5: A symbol incised on a piece of grey pottery belonging to *Dawenkou* culture.[13, 14]

5) *Erlitou*

Figure 1.6: Pottery inscriptions found from the archaeological site of *Erlitou* dated *c.* 1900–1500 BC.[14, 15]

Located 9 kilometres southwest of *Yanshi* of *Henan* province, dated *c.* 1900–1500 BC, and excavated from 1959, the archaeological site of *Erlitou* is an early Bronze Age society before the *Shang* dynasty.

The *Erlitou* culture is named after the site. Unearthed from the archaeological site of *Erlitou*, discoveries include the foundations of palatial buildings, paved roads, royal tombs, bronze foundries etc. Significantly, archaeologists have also found more than 24 pottery inscriptions.

Many scholars in China identify *Erlitou* with the *Xia* dynasty [16] — the earliest dynasty of the Three Dynasties (*Xia*, *Shang* and *Zhou*) mentioned in **Records of the Grand Historian of China** [17] by *Sima Qian* (*c*. 145 – 93 BC).

6) *Yinxu* (Ruins of *Yin*)

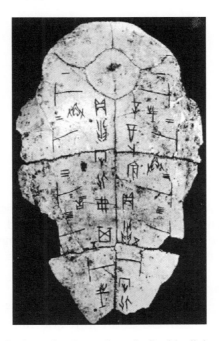

Figure 1.7: An inscribed tortoise shell with divination record
from *Yinxu, Anyang*.

Located near *Anyang* of *Henan* province, *Yinxu* was the capital of the *Yin* dynasty.[†] First excavated in 1928, since then, a massive number of tortoise shells and ox scapulae (which are generally referred to as oracle bones in the context of the ancient Chinese characters) have been unearthed from the site. So far some 4000

† *c*. 1300–1046 BC, the latter half of the *Shang* dynasty

characters (mainly incised on oracle bones) have been found, of which some 1300 characters have been recognized. The rich oracle bone inscriptions found in *Yinxu* attest to a very mature and nearly full Chinese writing system in use during the period of the *Shang* dynasty.[2, 3, 18–21]

Figure 1.8: An inscribed ox scapula, painted red, recording the social life, weather etc. of the *Shang* period, from *Yinxu*, *Anyang*. The scapula is 322mm long and 198mm wide, and contains more than 160 characters.

1.1.3 Observations and mysteries

From the above, it can be seen that character-like marks and signs on ancient artifacts, dated from *c.* 7000–5800 BC (see **Jiahu**) to *c.* 1900–1500 BC (see **Erlitou**), have been found at many archaeological sites in China. However, the scarcity of those mark/sign bearing artifacts makes it a mountainous, if not impossible, task to answer convincingly the questions asked at the beginning of this section: When and where did writing start to emerge in China? How did it develop into the oracle bone script of the *Shang* dynasty?

Having briefly looked at and been intrigued by the enigma of the origins of Chinese characters, you may find the following observations and mysteries interesting and challenging.

Observations

1) Using tortoise shells and ox scapulae as media for incising signs and symbols in China can now be traced back to some 8000 years ago.

2) The usage of signs (on oracle bones and pots) had been quite persistent in China for some 5000 years before the oracle bone script of the *Shang* dynasty.

3) The key features of *hanzi* — square shaped and composed of simple elements — can be identified from almost all the signs, symbols and characters on animal bones and pots excavated from the archaeological sites mentioned in this book.

4) From 1300BC to 5AD, the growth of Chinese characters was very slow, only one more character per year on average.[†]

5) So far there hasn't been any inscribed animal bone found dated between 6000 BC and the first half of the *Shang* dynasty in *Henan* or anywhere else in China.

6) The archaeological record in China has never had the intensive examination of those in countries such as Egypt and Greece.

Mysteries

1) As oracle bone script is a nearly full writing system, the important question one must ask is: how did it come into existence? Was it the natural end result of a protracted period of development? Did it emerge suddenly from some genius and radical design of one inventor or a group of people, driven by various factors and pressures, inspired and constrained by all available then (which may include, for instance, the writing media such as animal bones or bamboo, the writing tools, the existing symbols/signs, the language itself etc.)? Or was it something else?

2) How much does a legend reflect the facts? Is it possible that the legend that *Cang Jie* created Chinese characters around the 27th century BC has some truth in it? If so, what does it

---

[†] Refer to Figure 5.1 in Chapter 5 — **Chinese Characters in Use Today**.

tell us?

3) How do the development of a language and the emergence of characters/words to record language interact with each other?

4) Can other areas of study, such as psychology and mathematics, help to complement the lack of archaeological evidence?

It is rather unsettling to realize that, ultimately some mysteries may never be answered, and some hypotheses never proved. At the same time, it is certainly comforting to know that the above realization does not diminish human intrigue. The pursuit of the holy grail of the study of the Chinese writing system — the origins of *hanzi* — will never stop.

1.2 The Post Oracle Bone Script Development of *Hanzi*

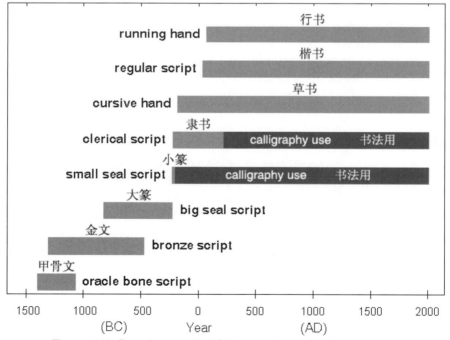

Figure 1.9: Development of Chinese characters from oracle bone script.

Oracle bone script dating from *c.* 1300BC during the period of the late *Shang* dynasty is a quite mature and nearly full writing system. As oracle bone inscriptions were incised with knives or other sharp instruments on tortoise shells and ox scapulae, characters in oracle bone script generally possess the following features (refer to Figures 1.7 and 1.8 for examples):

- Thin lines of various inclinations and sizes are the main elements in the majority of characters;
- Bending (changing of direction, via one execution or two executions of incising) is sharp;
- They are generally thin and tall, but not well spaced;
- They are mostly inconsistent in size and formation.

As depicted in Figure 1. 9 and will be shown in this section, Chinese characters as used today are the result of development, reform and standardization from oracle bone script after going through bronze script, big seal script, small seal script, clerical script, and regular script.

1.2.1 Bronze script

Figure 1.10: The inscription on the famous bronze vessel,
Dayu tripod, of the Western *Zhou* period. The vessel is kept
in the National Museum of China.

The *Zhou* dynasty replaced the *Shang* dynasty from 1066BC.

Both dynasties, the *Zhou* dynasty in particular, are famous for their bronze wares — symbol of divine power and royal right. The inscriptions engraved or cast on bronze wares, see Figure 1.10 for example, are called bronze script.

The earliest inscription bearing bronze wares unearthed so far are from the Ruins of *Yin* — the late *Shang* dynasty. It may well be possible that both oracle bone script and bronze script have the same origins. However, compared with the abundance of oracle bone inscriptions unearthed at the same site, it has been found that bronze inscriptions only started to flourish some 500 years later, and were at their peak during the time of the Western *Zhou* dynasty and the Spring and Autumn Period.

The early bronze script is actually very similar to oracle bone script, but the late bronze script is more developed and similar to big seal script. In both cases, as bronze inscriptions are engraved or cast on bronze wares, characters in bronze script generally have the following features:
- Lines are thicker;
- Bending is round and smooth;
- They appear tall and round, and compared with those in oracle bone inscriptions, are relatively well spaced.

1.2.2 Big seal script

Generally speaking, all the ancient scripts between oracle bone script and small seal script can be referred to as big seal script.

Specifically, the term big seal script is used to contrast with that of small seal script, and implies the script widely used within the *Qin* state during the Spring and Autumn Period and Warring States. It was developed from bronze script, but compared with those in bronze script, characters in big seal script have the following features:
- Lines are more controlled and smoother;
- Structure is neater and more conforming.

A good example of big seal script is the Stone Drum Inscription.

Figure 1.11: A small part of the inscription on one of the Stone Drums of *c.* 650 BC. The Stone Drums are kept in the Palace Museum of *Beijing*.

1.2.3 Small seal script

Figure 1.12: A small part of the Inscription of Mt. *Yi* Stele. The original stele was inscribed in 219 BC. The stele now kept in *Xi'an* Stele Forest Museum was carved in 993 AD (during the time of the *Song* dynasty) according to a rubbing from the original stele.

After the *Qin* state united China in 221 BC, under the first emperor *Qinshihuang*, there occurred a short period of reform and standardization of important things such as the units of currency and measurement, and the writing characters. The end result of reforming the writing characters was the adoption of small seal script and the abolition of many non-conforming characters. Compared with those in big seal script, characters in small seal script are:

- better shaped and of consistent sizes;
- simpler with a fixed form.

However, the adoption of small seal script didn't last long, except later on being employed as one of the artistic scripts of Chinese calligraphy, it ceased to be used in the *Han* dynasty.

A typical example of small seal script is the Inscription of Mountain (Mt.) *Yi* Stele.

1.2.4 Clerical script

Clerical script can be categorized into *Qin*-clerical script and *Han*-clerical script.

Qin-clerical script started to emerge from the *Qin* dynasty, and was actually used in parallel with small seal script at the time. Although small seal script was the 'official' writing script, the low-level clerks in the palace needed a simplified script to cut down their large amount of record-keeping and file-handling workloads. The most important change from small seal script was the adoption of sudden and angled change of writing direction (rather than via smooth rounding). This made writing faster and more convenient.

Han-clerical script, developed from small seal script and *Qin*-clerical script, introduced more reform, and became the main writing style during the *Han* dynasty. Apart from the changes witnessed in *Qin*-clerical script, Chinese characters experienced some other vital changes:

- Rather than tall and round, characters became squarer shaped;
- Many top-bottom structured characters became left-right

structured characters.

The key reason behind all the changes, from big/small seal script to clerical script, was to simplify and standardize Chinese characters, and to make writing more stroke based rather than drawing based. The emergence of clerical script marked a very important milestone in the development of *hanzi*, and laid the foundation of contemporary *hanzi*.

Figure 1.13: A small part of the inscription on *Cao Quan* Stele of the *Han* dynasty. The stele is now kept in *Xi'an* Stele Forest Museum.

Figure 1.13 presents 9 Chinese characters in clerical script from a famous stele.

1.2.5 Regular script

Starting to emerge from the end of the *Han* dynasty, descending from clerical script directly, and gradually maturing and becoming the de facto writing style during the *Sui* dynasty and the *Tang* dynasty, regular script:
- standardized all the basic strokes as used today;
- emphasized the symmetry of characters;
- made square-shaped the standard shape of *hanzi*.

Nowadays seal script and clerical script are only employed in Chinese calligraphy. Regular script is the standard writing style in print and daily hand-writing, whether employed in complex Chinese characters or simplified Chinese characters.

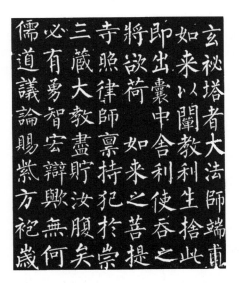

Figure 1.14: *Xuanmi* Pagoda Stele was erected in 841 (during the period of the *Tang* dynasty), and was inscribed in regular script by renowned calligrapher *Liu Gongquan*. The stele is now kept in *Xi'an* Stele Forest Museum.

More work in regular script can be found in Chapter 4 — **Writing Hanzi**.

1.2.6 Running hand and cursive hand

Unlike the seal, clerical and regular scripts, running hand and cursive hand are not different and independent scripts. They are two distinct writing styles employed in Chinese calligraphy, and they are also used in daily life.

Although the main aim of writing *hanzi* in running hand and cursive hand is to speed up writing by means of simplification and connectedness of strokes, when they are employed in ordinary daily writing, it is very important to ensure the readability of any manuscript.

Figure 1.15: Some characters from *'Lantingxu'*, which is a masterpiece in running hand by the calligrapher *Wang Xizhi* of the Eastern *Jin*. The original manuscript was lost during the *Tang* dynasty. The Palace Museum of *Beijing* keeps some copies of it made during the *Tang* dynasty by various calligraphers.

Figure 1.16: 'Four Ancient Poems' is a masterpiece in cursive hand by the calligrapher *Zhang Xu* of the *Tang* dynasty. The manuscript is now kept in the *Liaoning* Provincial Museum.

When running hand and cursive hand, cursive hand in particular, are employed in Chinese calligraphy work, the key is to try to express the abstraction and flow of the inscription.

1.3 The Classification of *Hanzi*

In this section, based on *Xu Shen*'s etymological dictionary **Shuowen Jiezi**, we shall examine the classification of *hanzi* from their etymological origins. Although this classification has its own limitations, it still remains an indispensable tool for anyone who is interested in associating and mapping the meanings of *hanzi* with their forms and configurations.

In **Shuowen Jiezi**, *Xu Shen* classified *hanzi* into six categories:
- pictographic characters
- ideographic characters
- associative compounds
- pictophonetic characters
- mutually explanatory characters
- phonetic loan characters

and categorized the collected 9353 characters as follows:

Category	Subtotal	Percentage (%)
Pictographic Characters	364	4
Ideographic Characters	125	1
Associative Compounds	1167	12
Pictophonetic Characters	7697	82

Table 1-1: Composition of 9353 Chinese characters in **Shuowen Jiezi**.

Pictographic and ideographic characters have evolved from the ancient pictographs and ideographs, and they form a very small portion of Chinese characters in use today. Pictophonetic characters make up the absolute majority of *hanzi* — some 80% [22] of contemporary Chinese characters are pictophonetic characters.

1.3.1 Pictographic characters

Pictographic characters represent specific objects, and they have evolved directly from ancient pictorial sources. The table below includes some examples of pictographic characters.

Pictorial	Character (Sound)	Meaning
	鸟 (*niǎo*)	bird
	鱼 (*yú*)	fish
	羊 (*yáng*)	goat
	日 (*rì*)	sun
	月 (*yuè*)	moon
	田 (*tián*)	field

	水 (shuǐ)	water
	山 (shān)	mountain

As it will be shown later in Section 1.4, by tracing back to their roots, you can see that some pictographic characters still in use today resemble, to some degree, the objects they represent.

1.3.2 Ideographic characters

Ideographic characters (which can also be referred to as self-explanatory characters) were originally used to convey ideas rather than objects, and they have evolved from abstract indicative symbols and pictorial sources that contained abstract indicative symbols.

The table below shows some examples.

Symbol/Pictorial	Character (Sound)	Meaning
▬ and ❙	一 (yī)	one
═ and ❙❙	二 (èr)	two
☰ and ❙❙❙	三 (sān)	three

	上 (*shàng*)	top, up
	下 (*xià*)	below, down
	大 (*dà*)	big, large
	本 (*běn*)	root (of tree)
	末 (*mò*)	tip (of tree)

1.3.3 Associative compounds

Associative compounds are also called 'compound indicatives'.

An associative compound is formed by combining two or more elements, each with a specific but subtle meaning, to create a new character and to represent a new meaning.

Let us examine the eight characters listed in the following table, and see how they are constructed:
1) 灭 (extinguish)
灭 (extinguish) consists of 火 (fire) underneath and '一' (one or just

a straight line) on top. If there were a fire, what would you do? Put something on top to stop it. That is 灭 (extinguish/put out).

Character (Meaning)	Main Element (Meaning)	Support Element (Meaning)	Sound (in *Pinyin*)
灭 (extinguish)	火 (fire)	一 (a straight line)	*miè*
灾 (disaster)	火 (fire)	宀 (roof)	*zāi*
林 (woods)	木 (tree)	木 (tree)	*lín*
森 (forest)	林 (woods)	木 (tree)	*sēn*
休 (rest)	亻 (person)	木 (tree)	*xiū*
歪 (crooked)	正 (straight)	不 (not, no)	*wāi*
解 (dissect)	刀 (knife)	牛角 (horn of ox)	*jiě*
鸣 (chirp)	鸟 (bird)	口 (mouth)	*míng*

2) 灾 (disaster)
灾 (disaster) consists of 火 (fire) underneath and '宀' on top, in which '宀' is the roof of a house or room (室). If a house caught on fire, it would certainly be a disaster (灾).

3) and 4) 林 (woods) and 森 (forest)
The basis of these two characters (林 and 森) is 木 (tree/wood). Two trees together form woods (林), and with another tree on top of woods (林) you have got a forest (森).

5) 休 (rest)
休 (rest) consists of '亻' (another form of 人 — person) and 木 (tree). When someone leans on a tree, they are likely to be resting.

6) 歪 (crooked)
歪 (crooked) consists of 正 (straight) and 不 (not, no). 'Not straight'

is therefore 'crooked'.

7) 解 (dissect)
解 (dissect) consists of three simple characters 角 (horn), 牛 (ox) and 刀 (knife), and it originally meant using a knife to dissect a horn from an ox.

8) 鸣 (chirp)
Putting 鸟 (bird) and 口 (mouth) together is probably the most simple and intuitive combination to indicate the sound of a bird — chirp.

1.3.4 Pictophonetic characters

Pictophonetic characters are also called 'phono-semantic compounds'.

A pictophonetic character generally consists of two parts: a semantic element (a pictographic or ideographic character, or its short form) to indicate the meaning, and a phonetic element (another pictographic or ideographic character, or its short form) to symbolize the sound of the constructed pictophonetic character.

Let us examine the eight pictophonetic characters listed in the table on the next page:
1) 氧 (oxygen)
It consists of two characters — 气 and 羊. The semantic part 气 (gas) is a pictographic character and used to indicate that the composed character is a type of gas; the phonetic part 羊 is pronounced *yáng* and used to give the sound of the composed character. It should be noted that, although the phonetic part 羊 (goat) is a pictographic character itself, it is used here only for the purpose of providing the sound.

2) 洋 (ocean)
It has the sound of its phonetic part 羊. Its semantic element '氵' is a short form of the character 水 (water).

3) 忘 (forget)
It sounds the same as its phonetic part 亡 (*wáng*) but with a

different tone. Its semantic element 心 (heart) indicates that 忘 (forget) is something that happens in people's hearts (mind).

4) 架 (rack/shelf)
Its semantic element is 木 (wood), and its phonetic element 加 is pronounced *jiā*.

Character (Meaning)	Semantic Element (Meaning)	Phonetic Element (Sound)	Sound (in *Pinyin*)
氧 (oxygen)	气 (air/gas)	羊 (*yáng*)	*yǎng*
洋 (ocean)	氵 (water)	羊 (*yáng*)	*yáng*
忘 (forget)	心 (heart)	亡 (*wáng*)	*wàng*
架 (rack/shelf)	木 (wood)	加 (*jiā*)	*jià*
转 (rotate)	车 (carriage)	专 (*zhuān*)	*zhuàn*
爬 (crawl)	爪 (claw)	巴 (*bā*)	*pá*
固 (solid)	囗 (enclosure)	古 (*gǔ*)	*gù*
闷 (stuffy)	心 (heart)	门 (*mén*)	*mèn*

5) 转 (rotate)
It has got two character parts — 车 and 专. Here 专 is the phonetic element and pronounced *zhuān*, and 车 is the semantic element. In Chinese, 车 has a few meanings, but they are all related to wheel or rotating.

6) 爬 (crawl)
Its semantic element 爪 means claw. 爬 (*pá*) and its phonetic element 巴 (*bā*) share the same vowel /a/.

7) 固 (solid)
It sounds the same as its phonetic part 古 (*gǔ*) but with a different

tone. Its semantic element □ means enclosure and solidifying.

8) 闷 (stuffy)
It sounds the same as its phonetic part 门 (*mén*) but with a different tone. Its semantic element 心 means heart.

According to the constitutional forms of their semantic elements ('pictures') and phonetic elements ('sounds'), pictophonetic characters can generally be classified into the following 10 groups:

(1) picture on the left and sound on the right, e.g. 灯, 材, 洋, 转, 驶, 晴, in which

$$灯 = 火 + 丁$$

(2) sound on the left and picture on the right, e.g. 攻, 救, 彩, 影, in which

$$救 = 求 + 攵$$

(3) picture on the top and sound at the bottom, e.g. 草, 星, 景, 袭, in which

$$星 = 日 + 生$$

(4) sound on the top and picture at the bottom, e.g. 架, 忘, 柔, 盒, 辈, in which

$$忘 = 亡 + 心$$

(5) picture outside and sound inside, e.g. 固, 围, 氧, 疼, 痛, in which

$$固 = 囗 + 古$$

(6) sound outside and picture inside, e.g. 闷, 舆, in which

$$闷 = 门 + 心$$

(7) picture in the corner, e.g. 旭, 匙, 修, in which

$$旭 = 九 + 日$$

(8) sound in the corner, e.g. 爬, 飓, 旗, 魅, in which

$$魅 = 鬼 + 未$$

(9) picture being separated by sound, e.g. 衷, 裹, 衔, in which

$$裹 = 衣 + 果$$

(10) sound being separated by picture, e.g. 辨, 辩, 瓣 have ' 刂' (knife), 'i ' (speech) and 瓜 (melon), respectively, in the middle

1.3.5 Mutually explanatory characters

Mutually explanatory characters normally have the same root, share the same semantic element, and are mutually explicable, but sound different.

For example, 老 (lǎo) and 考 (kǎo) are a pair of mutually explanatory characters.

1.3.6 Phonetic loan characters

A phonetic loan character is borrowed from an existing character (on the basis of sound) to represent a different meaning.

Take three Chinese characters 令 (lìng), 自 (zì) and 万 (wàn) for example. 令 is the Chinese character for 'order' and 'command', but it has also been borrowed to represent 'kind' and 'nice'. 自 originally meant 'nose', but later the character 鼻 was used for 'nose', and 自 was borrowed to mean 'self'. 万 originally meant 'scorpion', but later it was borrowed to mean 'ten thousand'.

1.4 The Roots of Some Pictographic and Ideographic *Hanzi*

Although pictographic and ideographic characters only make up a very small proportion of Chinese characters, they are nevertheless the core of *hanzi* as they constitute the main components of associative compounds and pictophonetic characters. It is therefore very important and useful not only to know them well but also to understand their roots.

Taking 18 pictographic and ideographic characters as examples, Figure 1.17 vividly depicts the development of these 18 characters.

	pictorial 图画	oracle bone script 甲骨文	bronze script 金文	seal script 篆书	regular script 楷书
人 human					
大 big, large					
天 sky					
目 eye					
口 mouth					
耳 ear					

(a) Characters derived from humans and the human body:
人，大，天，目，耳，口

	pictorial 图画	oracle bone script 甲骨文	bronze script 金文	seal script 篆书	regular script 楷书
日 sun					日
月 moon					月
山 mountain					山
水 water					水
土 soil					土
田 field					田

(b) Characters derived from nature: 日，月，山，水，土，田

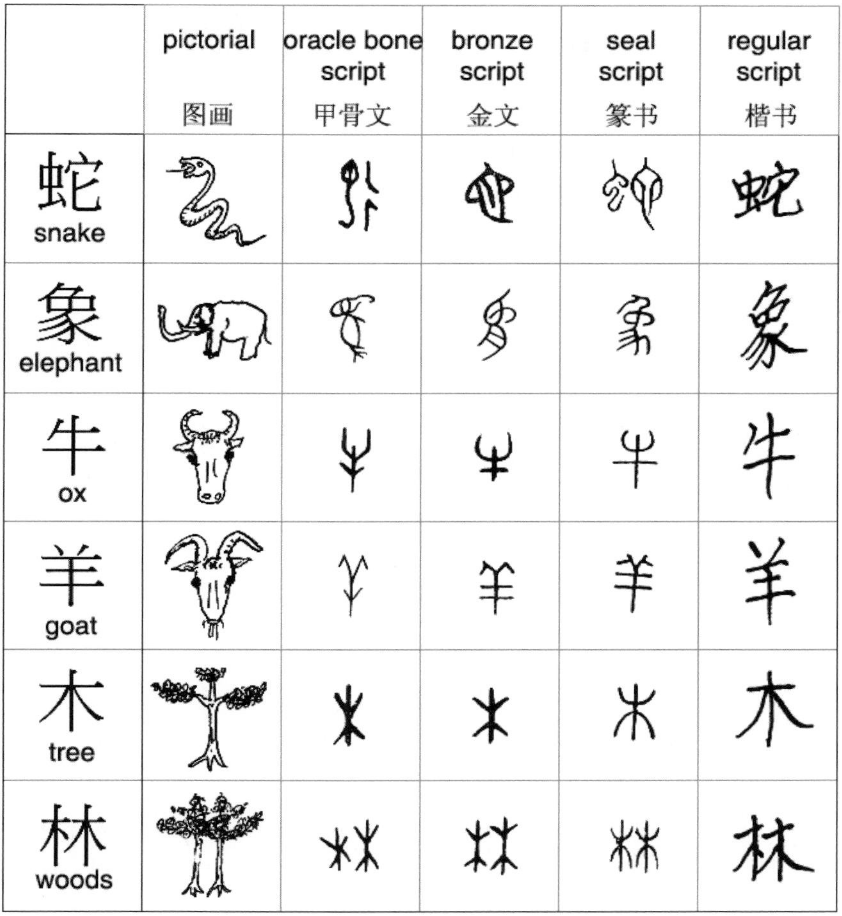

	pictorial 图画	oracle bone script 甲骨文	bronze script 金文	seal script 篆书	regular script 楷书
蛇 snake					
象 elephant					
牛 ox					
羊 goat					
木 tree					
林 woods					

(c) Characters derived from animals and trees/plants:
蛇，象，牛，羊，木，林

Figure 1.17: Roots of 18 pictographic and ideographic
characters.

Pronunciation of *Hanzi*
汉字的读音

2

"For me, words are a form of action, capable of influencing change. Their articulation represents a complete, lived experience."

Ingrid Bengis

Chinese characters — *hanzi* — do not themselves explicitly give information about their pronunciation. This is one of the reasons why it is difficult, at first, for native speakers of phonetic languages (such as English), to learn Chinese. To help pronounce Chinese characters correctly and easily, transcription systems have been devised to phonetically represent spoken Chinese. Using the Latin script to transcribe Chinese sounds is called 'romanization' or 'latinization'.

It is well known that Chinese is spoken in many different dialects, of which Mandarin, Cantonese and Shanghainese are three of the main ones. Mandarin is the standard spoken Chinese in the People's Republic of China, therefore it is called *putonghua* — literally 'common language'. It is also the largest first language in the world, and is spoken by some 1 billion people worldwide.[†] In this book, unless indicated otherwise, spoken Chinese means Mandarin.

The official romanization system adopted in China is *pinyin*, which means spelling. *Pinyin* is recognized by the United Nations and ISO (ISO-7098) as the standard romanization for Mandarin. The Wade-Giles system is another well-known romanization system for spoken Chinese, but has now been completely replaced by *pinyin* both inside and outside of China.

[†] The population in China as of 0:00 on 1st November 2005 stood at 1306.28 million.[1]

2.1 Chinese Phonetic Spelling System — *Pinyin*

Pinyin adopts the letters of the Latin alphabet as the phonemic symbols, and specifies the sounds of *hanzi* according to Mandarin. Based on a set of spelling rules, each Chinese character can then be given a phonetic notation. Therefore *pinyin* is the key to learning to speak Mandarin. Furthermore, when looking up an unknown character in a dictionary, one has to refer to its *pinyin* to be able to pronounce it. When typing Chinese characters into a computer, the *Pinyin* input method (see Chapter 7 — **Computer Processing of Chinese Characters**) is the easiest method.

2.1.1 Basic concepts

Syllable

It is defined as a unit of spoken language larger than a phoneme. English words can be one-syllable or multi-syllable. In Chinese, each character represents a syllable, and in most cases, it is a monosyllabic word — a word that only possesses one syllable (refer to Chapter 9 — **Chinese Words, Idioms and Proverbs**).

Tone

By definition, tone is the intonation contour of a syllable. In languages such as English, tone is not phonemic. In Chinese, however, tone is phonemic, and it is actually the intonation contour of a Chinese character.

1) four tones
Chinese characters can have four different tones: high-level (usually referred to as the 1st sound, marked by ' ¯ '), rising (the 2nd sound, marked by ' ´ '), fall-rise (the 3rd sound, marked by ' ˘ '), and falling (the 4th sound, marked by ' ˋ ').

Based on the contour and pitch of each tone, these four tones can be depicted by the four intonation contours as shown in Figure 2.1.

2) soft sound
Similar to unstressed syllables in English, some syllables in

Chinese are pronounced weakly and shortly. In these cases, the weakly and shortly pronounced syllable is said to be a soft sound. Soft sounds do not bear any tone marking (see the section **syllable structure and tone marking** below).

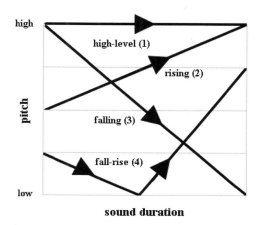

Figure 2.1: Four intonation contours of Chinese characters.

2.1.2 The phonetic symbols of pinyin

Within the tables in this section, apart from some Chinese characters (enclosed within curved brackets, e.g. {日}), you will also see *zhuyin* symbols (e.g. ㄚ and ㄨ).†

1) the alphabet of *pinyin*

Pinyin Symbol	A a	B b	C c	D d	E e	F f	G g
Name in *Zhuyin*	ㄚ	ㄅㄝ	ㄘㄝ	ㄉㄝ	ㄜ	ㄝㄈ	ㄍㄝ
Pinyin Symbol	H h	I i	J j	K k	L l	M m	N n
Name in *Zhuyin*	ㄏㄚ	ㄧ	ㄐㄧㄝ	ㄎㄝ	ㄝㄌ	ㄝㄇ	ㄋㄝ
Pinyin Symbol	O o	P p	Q q	R r	S s	T t	
Name in *Zhuyin*	ㄜ	ㄆㄝ	ㄑㄧㄡ	ㄚㄦ	ㄝㄙ	ㄊㄝ	
Pinyin Symbol	U u	V v #	W w	X x	Y y	Z z	
Name in *Zhuyin*	ㄨ	ㄞㄝ	ㄨㄚ	ㄒㄧ	ㄧㄚ	ㄗㄝ	

> # V is only used to spell sounds from foreign words, languages of national minorities and dialects in China.

---

† *Zhuyin* means annotating sounds. Different from the *pinyin* system, it mainly uses variant ancient characters to phonetically annotate Chinese sounds, especially Mandarin. In the PR China, it has been superseded by *pinyin*. In Taiwan, however, it is still the standard phonetic system.

2) consonants

b ㄅ {玻}	p ㄆ {坡}	m ㄇ {摸}	f ㄈ {佛}	d ㄉ {得}	t ㄊ {特}	n ㄋ {讷}	l ㄌ {勒}
g ㄍ {哥}	k ㄎ {科}	h ㄏ {喝}	j ㄐ {基}	q ㄑ {欺}	x ㄒ {希}		
zh ㄓ {知}	ch ㄔ {蚩}	sh ㄕ {诗}	r ㄖ {日}	z ㄗ {资}	c ㄘ {雌}	s ㄙ {思}	

3) vowels
3.1) simple vowels

a ㄚ {啊}	o ㄛ {喔}	e ㄜ {鹅}	i ㄧ {衣}	u ㄨ {乌}	ü ㄩ {迂}

3.2) compound vowels

	i ㄧ {衣}	u ㄨ {乌}	ü ㄩ {迂}
a ㄚ {啊}	ia ㄧㄚ {呀}	ua ㄨㄚ {蛙}	
o ㄛ {喔}		uo ㄨㄛ {窝}	
e ㄜ {鹅}	ie ㄧㄝ {耶}		eü ㄩㄝ {约}
ai ㄞ {哀}		uai ㄨㄞ {歪}	
ei ㄟ {诶}		uei ㄨㄟ {威}	
ao ㄠ {熬}	iao ㄧㄠ {腰}		
ou ㄡ {欧}	iou ㄧㄡ {忧}		
an ㄢ {安}	ian ㄧㄢ {烟}	uan ㄨㄢ {弯}	üan ㄩㄢ {冤}
en ㄣ {恩}	in ㄧㄣ {因}	uen ㄨㄣ {温}	ün ㄩㄣ {晕}
ang ㄤ {昂}	iang ㄧㄤ {央}	uang ㄨㄤ {汪}	
eng ㄥ {vowel of 亨}	ing ㄧㄥ {英}	ueng ㄨㄥ {翁}	
ong ㄨㄥ {vowel of 轰}	iong ㄩㄥ {雍}		

4) tone signs and marking (taking the vowel /a/ for example)

Tone Name	high-level	rising	fall-rise	falling
Common Name	1st sound	2nd sound	3rd sound	4th sound
Sign	‾	´	ˇ	ˋ
Marking	ā	á	ǎ	à

5) syllable-dividing mark

There is only one syllable-dividing mark in Chinese, that is /'/. For instance, *Xi'an* is the ancient Chinese city where you can see the famous terracotta army of the *Qin* dynasty.

2.1.3 Syllable structure and tone marking

Syllable structure

Syllable structure represents the make-up of a syllable, and it is about the sounds and their combination in a syllable.

A Chinese syllable basically has the following features:
1) There is always a tone except for soft sounds.
2) There is at least one vowel.
3) If there is more than one consonant, consonants can be put together.
4) Only consonants /n/ and /ng/ can be at the end of a syllable.
5) In most cases, a syllable begins with a consonant.

Syllable tone marking

Scheme for the Chinese Phonetic Alphabet [2] stipulates that the intonation mark symbols (tone signs) should be marked on top of the main vowel in a syllable. What if there are two or more vowels in a syllable? Which one is the main vowel? The answer is very simple: the main vowel is the most resounding one. That is, the vowel that requires you to open your mouth more than is necessary for the other vowels there.

As a matter of fact, among all the 6 simple vowels of *pinyin*, the most resounding one is /a/, next comes /o/ and /e/, and the least resounding ones are /i/, /u/ and /ü/.

To help memorize the tone marking rules summarized above, pupils in Chinese primary schools all know the following verse:

> Always use /a/ if it is there,
> Otherwise look for /o/ and /e/.
> Use the last one when /i/ and /u/ are together,
> But get rid of the dot in /i/ when it is to be marked.
> There will be no choice if there is only one vowel,
> And there will be no need of marking for soft sound.

2.2 Chinese Sounds In Terms of English Pronunciation

For the best effect, beginners should study this section in conjunction with audio materials of Mandarin Chinese sounds.[3]

It is worth emphasizing that, like any other language, Chinese has its own repertoire of sounds that cannot be matched up exactly with those of any other language. Using English sounds to resemble Mandarin Chinese sounds is only to help beginners with their initial familiarization of the Chinese language. If used inappropriately and taken as golden rules, such practice can give rise to unexpected and unpleasant effects — native Chinese speakers will find it hard to understand what you are conversing. The best practice, as with learning any other foreign language, is to take some Mandarin Chinese lessons, to spend some time watching Chinese TV or listening to Chinese radio, and to find opportunities to chat with native Chinese speakers.

Bearing this in mind, the tables below try to give the best approximations for the majority of Mandarin Chinese sounds. However, as you will see, four special Chinese consonants — /j/, /q/, /r/ and /x/ — have not been given any approximations. The reason for this is very simple: there are no close English sounds for them, and the ways in which they are pronounced are so different from those in which English sounds are normally made. For these 4 'tricky' sounds, anatomical and linguistic descriptions will be adopted. For beginners, when faced with such difficult sounds, it is always very tempting to rely only on 'similar' native sounds, which are often provided in many web sites and Chinese language text books. However one has to put this into perspective and be aware of the potential misleading effect of such short cut practice.

Syllables in Chinese normally consist of two parts: initial — the consonant at the beginning of a syllable, and final — the remainder of a syllable.

2.2.1 When approximations can be made

The tables below include 23 initials and 35 finals, but the approximations are given only for 19 initials and 35 finals.

Initial	Sound Approximation	Examples
b	[b]ird	爸 (dad) — *bà*; 冰 (ice) — *bīng*
p	[p]en	怕 (fear) — *pà*; 跑 (run) — *pǎo*
m	[m]other	妈 (mum) — *mā*; 猫 (cat) — *māo*
f	[f]an	飞 (fly) — *fēi*; 富 (rich) — *fù*
d	[d]iet	大 (large) — *dà*; 东 (east) — *dōng*
t	[t]ea	天 (sky) — *tiān*; 头 (head) — *tóu*
n	[n]ice	脑 (brain) — *nǎo*; 鸟 (bird) — *niǎo*
l	[l]ist	泪 (tear) — *lèi*; 聋 (deaf) — *lóng*
g	[g]ap	高 (high) — *gāo*; 骨 (bone) — *gǔ*
k	[k]ind	开 (open) — *kāi*; 空 (empty) — *kōng*
h	[h]elp	好 (good) — *hǎo*; 火 (fire) — *huǒ*
j	N/A; see later	家 (home) — *jiā*; 脚 (foot) — *jiǎo*
q	N/A; see later	妻 (wife) — *qī*; 桥 (bridge) — *qiáo*
x	N/A; see later	想 (think) — *xiǎng*; 小 (small) — *xiǎo*
zh	[dr]aw	炸 (fry) — *zhá*; 猪 (pig) — *zhū*
ch	[ch]urch	吃 (eat) — *chī*; 春 (spring) — *chūn*
sh	[sh]ow	手 (hand) — *shǒu*; 山 (mountain) — *shān*
r	N/A; see later	人 (human) — *rén*; 日 (sun) — *rì*
z	see[ds]	灾 (disaster) — *zāi*; 左 (left) — *zuǒ*
c	ca[ts]	雌 (female) — *cí*; 醋 (vinegar) — *cù*
s	[s]mile	丝 (silk) — *sī*; 算 (calculate) — *suàn*
y [†]	[y]es	右 (right) — *yòu*; 易 (easy) — *yì*
w [‡]	[w]ine	胃 (stomach) — *wèi*; 午 (noon) — *wǔ*

Final	Sound Approximation	Examples
a	f[a]ther	法 (law) — *fǎ*
o	s[aw]	佛 (Buddha) — *fó*
e	h[er] (without r sound)	喝 (drink) — *hē*
i	s[ee]	力 (force) — *lì*; 易 (easy) — *yì* †
u	f[oo]l	醋 (vinegar) — *cù*; 赌 (bet) — *dǔ*
ü	German [ü]ben; French t[u]	女 (woman) — *nǚ* #; 婿 (son-in-law) — *xù* #
ai	[ai]sle	灾 (disaster) — *zāi*
ei	[ei]ght	胃 (stomach) — *wèi*
ao	c[ow]	高 (high) — *gāo*
ou	s[o]	头 (head) — *tóu*
an	c[an]	烟 (smoke) — *yān*
en	tak[en]	人 (human) — *rén*
ang	[ang]st	想 (think) — *xiǎng*
eng	*e* + si[ng]	风 (wind) — *fēng*
ong	*u* + si[ng]	聋 (deaf) — *lóng*
ia	*i* + *a* ([ya]rd)	家 (home) — *jiā*; 牙 (tooth) — *yá* †
ie	*i* + *e* ([ye]t)	猎 (hunt) — *liè*; 夜 (night) — *yè* †
iao	*i* + *ao*	小 (small) — *xiǎo*; 药 (medicine) — *yào* †
iou (*iu*)	*i* + *ou*	牛 (ox) — *niú* §; 右 (right) — *yòu* †
ian	*i* + *an* ([yen])	天 (sky) — *tiān*; 盐 (salt) — *yán* †
in	sh[een]	新 (new) — *xīn*; 银 (silver) — *yín* †
iang	*i* + *ang*	想 (think) — *xiǎng*; 洋 (ocean) — *yáng* †
ing	s[ing]	冰 (ice) — *bīng*; 硬 (hard) — *yìng* †
iong	*i* + *ong*	穷 (poor) — *qióng*; 用 (use) — *yòng* †
ua	*u* + *a* ([wah])	花 (flower) — *huā*; 挖 (dig) — *wā* ‡
uo	*u* + s[aw]	左 (left) — *zuǒ*; 卧 (lie) — *wò* ‡
uai	*u* + *ai*	坏 (bad) — *huài*; 外 (outer) — *wài* ‡
uei (*ui*)	*u* + *ei*	对 (correct) — *duì* §; 胃 (stomach) — *wèi* ‡
uan	*u* + *an*	关 (close) — *guān*; 弯 (bend) — *wān* ‡
uen (*un*)	*u* + *en*	春 (spring) — *chūn* §; 温 (warm) — *wēn* ‡

uang	*u* + *ang*	光 (light) — *guāng*; 网 (net) — *wǎng* ‡
ueng	*u* + *eng*	瓮 (urn) — *wēng* ‡
üe	*i* + *e*	掠 (plunder) — *lüě* #; 雪 (snow) — *xuě* #
üan	*ü* + *an*	猿 (ape) — *yuán* †
ün	*ü* + *n*	云 (cloud) — *yún* †

† *y* is placed before syllables starting with *i* and *ü*, and *i* is omitted if it is followed by another vowel and *ü* is replaced by *u*.

‡ *w* is placed before syllables starting with *u*, and *u* is omitted if it is not the last vowel.

ü is replaced by *u* when it is preceded by *j*, *q* and *x*, but stays unchanged after *l* and *n*.

§ When preceded by a consonant, *iou*, *uei* and *uen* are written as *iu*, *ui* and *un*, respectively.

With the help of the English words from the above tables, now you can try to spell and say the following Chinese characters in Mandarin.

Practice 1: 妈 (mum) — *mā*

m + a [m]other f[a]ther	

Practice 2: 爸 (dad) — *bà*

b + a [b]ird f[a]ther	

Practice 3: 手 (hand) — *shǒu*

sh + o [sh]ow s[o]	

Practice 4: 天 (sky) — *tiān*

t + i + an [t]ea l[i]st c[an]	

Practice 5: 谁 (who) — *shuí*

sh + oo + ei		
[sh]ow f[oo]l [ei]ght		

Practice 6: 光 (light) — *guāng*

g + oo + ang		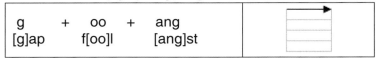
[g]ap f[oo]l [ang]st		

2.2.2 The sounds of /j/, /q/, /r/ and /x/

These four tricky sounds can only be initials in Chinese syllables.

/j/, /q/ and /x/ are all 'palatal consonants' and are articulated with the body of the tongue raised close to the hard palate — the middle part of the roof of the mouth. The differences among them are:
- /j/ is an unaspirated sound;
- /q/ is an aspirated sound;
- /x/ is a voiceless fricative sound.

To make the /j/ and /q/ sounds, raise the tongue close to the palate, then let the air break the blockage and flow out with friction. /j/ is articulated with weak air and is unaspirated; /q/ is articulated with strong air and is aspirated. The /x/ sound is articulated with the tongue raised close to the palate and the air streamed out of the narrow channel with friction.

/r/ is a 'retroflex consonant'. To make the /r/ sound, let the tip of the tongue curl back close to the palate, and the air flow out the narrow space with voice.

2.3 Illustrations of Tone Variations in Chinese Sentences and Poems

Non-Chinese speakers always say that Chinese sounds musical when they begin to learn Chinese. To non-native speakers, the same can actually be said about all languages. However, as

Chinese characters have four different tones, the variation of tones in a Chinese sentence or poem is very unique, rich and hence music-like.

To best illustrate the unique music-like tone variations in Chinese sentences and poems, the tone variations in sentences can be learned intuitively, when they are depicted convincingly within the 'five horizontal lines' of a 5-line staff, see the examples below.

Example 1: some simple phrases

Phrase	*Pinyin*	Tone Variation
你好 (Hello)	*ní hǎo*	
早上好 (Good morning)	*zǎo shàng hǎo*	
晚上好 (Good evening)	*wǎn shàng hǎo*	
再见 (Bye)	*zài jiàn*	

Example 2: the poem 'Written on the Wall at West Forest Temple'

Poem and *pinyin*:

题西林壁
(宋，苏轼)

横看成岭侧成峰 (*héng kàn chéng lǐng cè chéng fēng*)，
远近高低各不同 (*yuǎn jìn gāo dī gè bù tóng*)。
不识庐山真面目 (*bù shí lú shān zhēn miàn mù*)，
只缘身在此山中 (*zhǐ yuán shēn zài cǐ shān zhōng*)。

Translation:

Written on the Wall at West Forest Temple
by *Su Shi* of the *Song* dynasty

Ridges join across
And peaks compete sideways,
Far and near, high and low — all different.
The reason you cannot fully appreciate
The truly spectacular view of Mt. *Lushan*:
You are deep inside the mountain.

Tone variation:

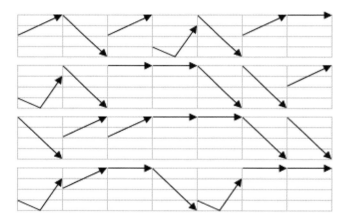

Example 3: the poem 'Climbing the Tower of Oriental Stork'

Poem and *pinyin*:

登鹳雀楼
(唐，王之涣)

白日依山尽 (*bái rì yī shān jìn*)，
黄河入海流 (*huáng hé rù hǎi liú*)。
欲穷千里目 (*yù qióng qiān lǐ mù*)，
更上一层楼 (*gèng shàng yī céng lóu*)。

Translation:

Climbing the Tower of Oriental Stork
by *Wang Zhihuan* of the *Tang* dynasty

The bright sun falls behind the mountains,
The Yellow River runs into the sea.
We widen our views three hundred miles by ascending one flight of stairs.

Tone variation:

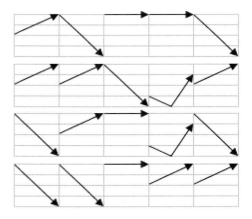

The Structure of Chinese Characters

汉字的字形

3

"The most general law in nature is equity — the principle of balance and symmetry which guides the growth of forms along the lines of the greatest structural efficiency."
Sir Herbert Edward Read (Anarchy and Order)

Unlike the characters in Indo-European languages, Chinese characters are two-dimensional [†] in nature and they have a unique and logical structure. This structure is a three-level hierarchy — entirety, components and strokes, entirety being the core.

The importance of understanding the structure of Chinese characters can never be over emphasized. Without basic knowledge about the structure of *hanzi*, one would neither be able to look up an unknown character from a Chinese dictionary (see Chapter 6 — **Looking up Characters in a Dictionary**), nor be able to write Chinese well (see Chapter 4 — **Writing *Hanzi***), and would certainly feel it a huge, if not impossible, task to learn and master the majority of the 2500 most frequently used characters as listed in Appendix I.

[†] In Indo-European languages, words are composed linearly from individual letters. Although Chinese characters are all square-shaped, the arrangement of strokes in a *hanzi* is complicated. As the arrangement of strokes in a *hanzi* is not confined in one direction, we say that Chinese characters possess a two-dimensional structure.

3.1 Strokes of Chinese Characters

Dissembling *hanzi* into their smallest elements, all Chinese characters are made up of strokes. There are altogether 28 different strokes, of which 8 strokes are the basic ones and the others are derived from them. See Table 3-2 and Table 3-3 for detail.

The constitution of *hanzi* is very precise. When engaged in writing a Chinese character, one should pay special attention to the accuracy and small details — how many strokes it contains, what these strokes are and where they are rendered within the character. Sometimes, the slightest change in length or position of a stroke can produce a totally different character. To best demonstrate the importance of precision in Chinese characters, the table below shows 14 pairs of similar looking but completely different characters.

入 (enter)	人 (human, people, person)
刀 (knife)	力 (force, power)
日 (sun; day, daytime)	曰 (say, speak)
儿 (child; son)	几 (table; a few)
手 (hand)	毛 (fur, hair)
天 (sky; day)	夭 (young; die young)
心 (heart; mind)	必 (must; certainly)
三 (three)	川 (river)
犬 (dog)	太 (very, extremely)
玉 (jade; beautiful)	主 (master; main)
己 (self, oneself)	已 (already; stop)
已 (already; stop)	巳 (the hours from 9 to 11 am)
于 (in, at; for)	干 (do; dried)
木 (tree, wood)	本 (root, origin)

Table 3-1: Examples of similar looking but completely different Chinese characters.

Order	Stroke	Name	Example
1	一	dash (one)	三 (three)
2	丨	perpendicular dash (line)	十 (ten)
3	丿	down stroke to the left (slash)	八 (eight)
4	丶	dot	方 (square)
5	ㄱ	bend	口 (mouth)
6	㇏	wavelike stroke	人 (person)
7	㇀	upstroke to the right	虫 (insect)
8	亅	hook	水 (water)

Table 3-2: 8 basic strokes of Chinese characters.

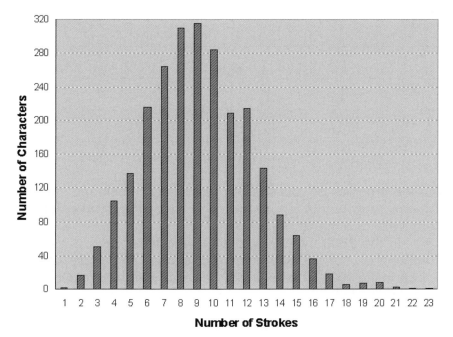

Figure 3.1: Characters grouped by number of strokes within the 2500 most frequently used characters.

Order	Stroke	Example	Order	Stroke	Example
1	㇆	又	14	㇄	弓
2	㇀	买	15	㇜	女
3	㇔	计	16	㇈	公
4	㇆	朵	17	㇟	代
5	㇉	九	18	㇉	家
6	㇌	队	19	㇆	同
7	㇉	及	20	㇂	风
8	㇌	乃	**shaped strokes**		
9	㇍	凸	1	一	千
10	㇗	民	2	丿	月
11	㇄	山	3	㇀	小
12	㇗	儿	4	㇇	之
13	㇞	专	5	丶	不

Table 3-3: 20 derived strokes of Chinese characters.

With the progress of your reading through this book and studying Chinese, you would appreciate the following stroke related characteristics of *hanzi:*

•   In the 2500 most frequently used characters, as listed in Appendix I, the average number of strokes in a single *hanzi* is 9.17; in the 1000 high frequency characters, the average number goes down to 8.03.

•   From Figure 3.1, it also can be found that, in the 2500 most frequently used characters, 9-stroke and 8-stroke characters are most popular — 316 and 310 characters respectively, and together they make a quarter of these 2500 characters.

A Note on Stroke Classification

The classification of strokes as shown in Table 3-2 and Table 3-3 is commonly referred to as '8-stroke classification' (because of 8 basic strokes), and it has been used and taught to school children for many centuries. To facilitate the computer processing and keyboard input of *hanzi* (refer to Chapter 7), a new classification called '5-stroke classification' was proposed in 1988 by China National Language and Character Working Committee.[1] Instead of having the 8 basic strokes and 20 derived strokes of Table 3-2 and Table 3-3, the '5-stroke classification' includes only 5 basic strokes, which are the first 5 strokes in Table 3-2. All the other strokes have been re-classified into these 5 strokes: wavelike stroke is now classified as dot, upstroke to right as dash, hook as perpendicular dash, and any bend-containing stroke (in Table 3-3) as bend. The new classification also assigns an order to these 5 strokes: dash, perpendicular dash, down stroke to the left, dot and bend. The order assignment within the '5-stroke classification' allows groups of characters with the same number of strokes to be ordered according to the assignment.

In comparison, the '5-stroke classification' is not as intuitive and natural as the '8-stroke classification'. To the beginners of Chinese study, it makes more sense and is more effective to start with the '8-stroke classification'. Once the '8-stroke classification' has been mastered, it is just a simple matter of switching and familiarization to work with the '5-stroke classification'.

3.2 The Components of *Hanzi*

All *hanzi* are made up of components. These components are the independent small units in Chinese characters. All components, except for one-stroke components such as '一' and '乙', are made up of multiple strokes.

Take the Chinese characters 姻 (marriage; relation by marriage) and 毁 (damage; destroy) for example, the relationships among strokes, components and the characters can be demonstrated via Figure 3.2.

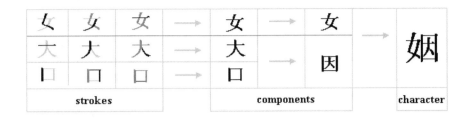

Figure 3.2(a): Relationship among strokes, components and
the character '姻'.

Figure 3.2(b): Relationship among strokes, components and
the character '毁'.

In the 3500 characters of frequent use, there are 384 different components; in the 1000 high frequency characters, there are 285 components. Table 3-4 lists the 86 main character-components (components that are characters themselves) that appear in the 1000 high frequency characters.

一	二	十	厂	七
one	two	ten	factory	seven
八	人	入	几	九
eight	man	enter	several	nine
儿	刀	力	又	了
son	knife	power	again	finish
于	才	及	门	也
at	ability	reach	gate	too
女	子	丰	天	专
woman	child	abundant	sky	specialize
五	车	比	日	中
five	cart	compare	sun	middle
内	见	手	毛	长
inner	see	hand	fur	long

片	为	心	巴	以
slice	for	heart	python	use
书	水	世	东	北
book	water	world	east	north
目	且	田	由	电
eye	and	field	reason	electricity
史	央	四	乎	乐
history	entreat	four	exhale	smile
永	必	司	民	出
forever	must	manage	people	exit
皮	发	母	耳	西
skin	hair	mother	ear	west
而	虫	年	农	争
but	insect	year	agriculture	contend
更	两	求	里	我
change	two	request	lining	I, me
身	局	其	事	雨
body	compel	that	thing	rain
非	革	面	重	象
non-	leather	face	heavy	elephant
黑				
black				

Table 3-4: 86 main character-components, and their meaning,
out of the 1000 high frequency characters.

3.3 Entirety of *Hanzi*

The entirety of *hanzi* means the 'harmoniously arranged skeleton'
nature of Chinese characters, and implies that the arrangement
and composition of strokes and components all follow certain
principles which will be discussed and demonstrated later. It
emphasizes the importance of long/short, thick/thin, bending/lifting
and expansion/contraction of strokes; it also shows the importance
of wide/narrow, large/small, high/low, spacious/dense and
dominant/recessive in components.

It is not hard to appreciate the importance of the 'harmoniously
arranged skeleton'. Given the fact that there are thousands of
different Chinese characters and each of them has its own unique
structure and composition, it is impossible to imagine writing them
distinctly, without the guidance of the 'harmoniously arranged
skeleton'.

3.3.1 Single-component characters

These characters themselves can be components, and they only consist of strokes.

The 'harmoniously arranged skeleton' for these characters involves three main principles: 1) a stationary 'centre of gravity'; 2) proportional strokes; and 3) controlled variations.

Stationary 'centre of gravity'

Where is the 'centre of gravity' of a *hanzi*? Metaphorically speaking, the 'centre of gravity' of a *hanzi* is the centre point of 'weight' of that *hanzi*. Once the 'centre of gravity' of a *hanzi* is located accurately, all its strokes should be arranged around it, and the character will seem balanced.

When a character has got mirror-symmetry, its centre of gravity will naturally be on the axis of symmetry. Some characters have their axis of symmetry through the central perpendicular-dash, for example: 串, 干, 申. Some characters have their axis of symmetry through the intersection point of two curved strokes, for example: 大, 又, 大, 天.

Characters such as 么, 刃, 乒 may not necessarily have their centres of gravity located on any of their strokes.

Proportional strokes

For all the strokes in a character, their styles and positions should be well adjusted, and their sizes should be in proportion. How? The following examples demonstrate the basic principles.

1) thick and thin in moderation
It would be reasonable for characters with fewer strokes, such as 大, 口, 上, to have slightly bolder and thicker strokes, and for characters with more strokes, such as 鬼 and 象, to have slightly

thinner and delicate strokes.

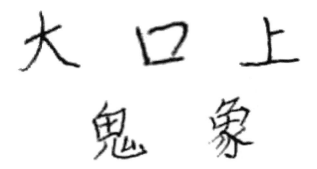

2) appropriate spaciousness

In characters such as 王, 主, 生, 丰, where dashes are stacked together horizontally, and in characters such as 川, 册, 山, 而, where perpendicular dashes stand close together, it is very important to keep appropriate spaces between the parallel strokes.

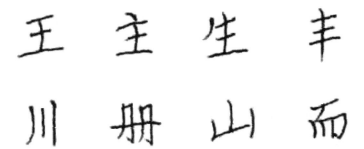

3) visual symmetry

In characters with intrinsic symmetry, such as 显, 苗, 日, it is necessary to visualize the symmetry.

4) stabilized supporting frame
In characters such as 人, 文, 犬, in which two curved strokes form the supporting frame of a character, it will help to 'stabilize' the characters if the two strokes: a) intersect at the 'centre of gravity'; b) are split at the appropriate angle; and c) are the correct length.

5) contracted surrounding frame
In framed characters such as 田, 日, 目, 国, where the surrounding frame controls the size, it is important to keep the surrounding frame contracted.

Controlled variations

1) enlarging and contracting
Take the character 三 for example: the top dash is of normal length; the middle dash is shorter than the top one, the result of contracting; the bottom dash is the longest one, the result of enlarging. The sample below also includes the characters 王 and 主.

2) inclined and straight
Take the character 十 for example: the dash could be inclined ever so slightly upwards from left to right (when we are writing it by hand); however the perpendicular dash should be kept straight upright. The sample below also includes the character 大.

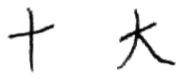

3) initiating and ending
Take the character 心 for example: the dot on the left initiates the character, the dot in the centre acts as a linking point, and the dot on the right ends the character. Some symmetry can be observed between the left and right dots.

4) dominant and recessive

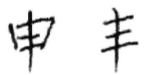

Take the character 申 for example: the central perpendicular dash is the main stroke, and therefore it should be relatively longer than the other strokes. The sample below also includes the character 丰.

3.3.2 Multi-component characters

Multi-component characters (or composite characters) all consist of two or more components.

The 'harmoniously arranged skeleton' for these characters indicates the deployment and assembly relationships and principles among all the constructing components.

Left and right structure ( )

How they are deployed	Examples
evenly	颜，顺，材
larger left	尉，鄢，敬
smaller left	信，清，惨
taller left	和，叙，扫
shorter left	呼，境，晚

Left, middle and right structure ( )

How they are deployed	Examples
evenly	糊，树，脚
unevenly	猴，谢，滩

Top and bottom structure ( )

How they are deployed	Examples
evenly	架，怒，契
larger top	感，型，盒
smaller top	岩，骂，昆
wider top	冒，告，胃
narrower top	畏，是，最

Top, middle and bottom structure ( )

How they are deployed	Examples
evenly	竟，蓝，鼻
unevenly	壶，褒，亨

Closed surrounding structure ( )

How they are deployed	Examples
contracted	国，围，团，图，园

Open surrounding structure ( )

How they are deployed	Examples
top left ( )	康，厨，病
bottom left ( )	进，赶，处
top right ( )	习，勾，或
top, left and bottom ( )	医，匪，匹
left, bottom and right ( )	画，函，凶
left, top and right ( )	网，风，闻

Writing *Hanzi*
汉字的书写

4

"Art strives for form, and hopes for beauty."
George W. Bellows

There are two types of *hanzi* writing: practical writing and artistic writing.

The two-dimensional nature of *hanzi* makes writing well a delicate and demanding task. However, with the grasp of the structure of Chinese characters and with practice, writing *hanzi* can certainly be perfected. A beautifully handwritten piece of Chinese work (a memo, essay, article …) will always be attractive to the intended readers, and can stimulate one's imagination from the content on paper to vivid pictures.

Some readers may wonder: nowadays, with the widespread use of modern computers, PDAs (Personal Digital Assistants), and MDAs (Mobile Digital Assistants), is handwriting important or necessary at all? My answer to the question is: yes, it is. I have three arguments: 1) it reflects who we are as individuals; 2) handwriting (*hanzi*) is like painting, it is an artistic and creative activity; 3) a simple and convincing comparison can be made to walking — with so many modern modes of transport, people still like and need to walk.

4.1 Daily Practical Writing

Daily practical writing covers a very broad spectrum of daily life and business activities — writing diaries, taking notes, writing letters, filling in forms, taking exams, drafting a plan/report/summary etc.

There are two main script styles adopted in daily practical writing — the regular script and the running hand. Because of the complicated two-dimensional form of Chinese characters, when engaged in writing, it is advisable that one should always follow the 'stroke order principles' in all scripts but one. The only exception is when writing characters in the cursive hand, which will be discussed in detail later.

4.1.1 Writing hanzi in the regular script

When writing *hanzi* in the regular script, the following 'stroke order principles' should be observed and complied with (refer to Table 4-1):

1) from top to bottom
2) from left to right
3) dash first, perpendicular dash last
4) down stroke to the left first, wavelike stroke to the right second
5) dash first, down stroke to the left second
6) main body first, dot last
7) middle first, then left and right sides
8) outside first, inside last
9) entering first, then closing the door behind you

Principle	Example Character	Writing Sequence		
from top to bottom	音	丶	立	音
from left to right	湘	氵	沐	湘
dash first, perpendicular dash last	丰	三	丰	
down stroke to the left first, wavelike stroke to the right second	八	丿	八	
dash first, down stroke to the left second	厂	一	厂	

main body first, dot last	太	大	太	
middle first, then left and right sides	水	亅	水	
outside first, inside last	同	冂	同	
entering first, then closing the door behind you	国	冂	国	国

Table 4-1: Examples demonstrating the stroke order
principles for writing *hanzi*.

The main part of the above 9 stroke order principles can be easily memorized with the help of the following ragged verse:[†]

字的写法在笔顺，
要领掌握笔生韵。
先横后竖上到下，
先撇后捺左右论。
从外到内谐又准，
最后关门字秀俊。

When literally translated, it reads:
> Stroke order is the key to writing *hanzi*,
> Once the principles are mastered the pen will run with rhyme.
> Dash first perpendicular stroke last, from top to bottom;
> Down stroke to left first wavelike stroke to right last, from left to right.
> Outside first inside last will help to be harmonious and accurate,
> Closing the door in the end will make an elegant *hanzi*.

Besides following the above stroke order principles, during writing, one should also always bear in mind the harmoniously arranged skeleton principles discussed in Chapter 3 — **The Structure of Chinese Characters**.

To write *hanzi* well, it is also very helpful to understand and appreciate the following tips:
1) strokes to be standardized
2) structure to be harmonized
3) composition to be internally compact
4) outline to be a square

[†] Adapted from the well known 'stroke order verse'.[1]

To demonstrate the tips discussed so far, two calligraphy works in the regular script are presented below, in which two different poems have been used.

Example 4.1 poem written on '田' grid paper:

Note: poem by *Wang Zhihuan*, a famous poet of the *Tang* dynasty.

Example 4.2 poem written on square-grid paper:

	静	夜	思	
		李	白	
床	前	明	月	光
疑	是	地	上	霜
举	头	望	明	月
低	头	思	故	乡

Note: poem by *Li Bai*, a renowned poet of the *Tang* dynasty.

4.1.2 Writing hanzi in the running hand

With regard to stroke order, structural composition etc., writing *hanzi* in the running hand is no different from writing *hanzi* in the regular script. However, when writing *hanzi* in the running hand, one has more freedom and flexibility with the drawing of strokes, the stroke style, and the structural layout.

Example 4.3 writing horizontally:

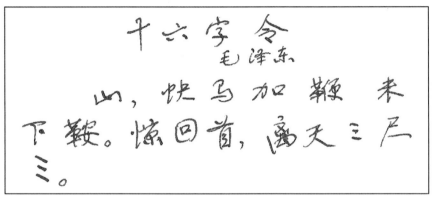

Note: poem by *Mao Zedong*, one of the main founders of the People's Republic of China, a poet and calligrapher.

In regular script and print form, the above poem reads:

十六字令

毛泽东

山，快马加鞭未下鞍。惊回首，离天三尺三。

In the next two examples, Example 4.4(a) and Example 4.4(b), each poem is written vertically (from right to left), and is presented in regular script and print form.

Example 4.4(a) writing vertically (from right to left):

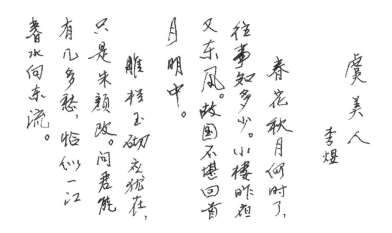

Note: poem by *Li Yu*, a poet and the last ruler of the Southern *Tang* Kingdom during the Five Dynasties and Ten Kingdoms Period.

虞美人
李煜

春花秋月何时了，
往事知多少。小楼昨夜
又东风，故国不堪回首
月明中。

雕栏玉砌应犹在，
只是朱颜改。问君能
有几多愁，恰似一江
春水向东流。

Example 4.4(b) writing vertically (from right to left):

Note: poem by *Lu You*, a famous poet of the Southern *Song* dynasty.

钗头凤

陆游

红酥手，黄藤酒，
满城春色宫墙柳。
东风恶，欢情薄，
一怀愁绪，几年离索。
错、错、错！

春如旧，人空瘦，
泪痕红邑鲛绡透。
桃花落，闲池阁。
山盟虽在，锦书难托。
莫、莫、莫！

4.2 Artistic Writing

The art of writing *hanzi* is called calligraphy, and is enjoyed by people from all walks of life. The popular calligraphic styles include the clerical script, cursive hand and seal script, with the latter two being most popular.

Example 4.5 (a) writing horizontally in the cursive hand:

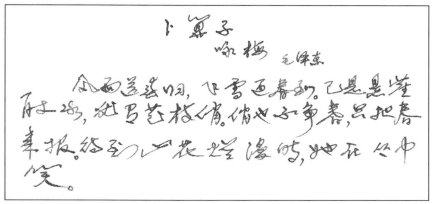

Note: poem by *Mao Zedong*.

In regular script and print form, the poem reads:

卜算子
咏梅
毛泽东

风雨送春归，飞雪迎春到。已是悬崖百丈冰，犹有花枝俏。
俏也不争春，只把春来报。待到山花烂漫时，她在<u>丛</u>中笑。

To excel at Chinese calligraphy normally takes years of practice, and it is worth memorizing and gradually absorbing the following metaphorical saying:

篆书如圈，隶书如蚕，楷书如立，行书如行，草书如跑。

The saying originated from *Su Shi*, often referred to as *Su Dongpo*, a renowned writer, poet, artist and calligrapher of the *Song* dynasty. When translated literally, it reads:

> Writing Chinese is as
> drawing circles in seal script,
> drawing silkworms in clerical script,
> standing firm in regular script,
> walking in running hand,
> running in cursive hand.

The saying may not sound as practical as all the tips and principles discussed in this chapter, but for someone who has been practising calligraphy long enough, it gradually makes increasing sense.

Writing *hanzi* in the cursive hand emphasizes the following points:
- Pay attention to details in strokes — mellow and full, connected and smooth;
- Strive to present the momentum and expression of the whole character;
- If necessary, break some of the rules mentioned earlier.

Example 4.5 (b) writing vertically (from right to left) in the cursive hand:

Note: the same poem as the second writing in Example 4.4.
Please compare them.

Example 4.6 writing vertically (from right to left), in the regular script and cursive hand, respectively:

沁园春雪

毛泽东

北国风光，千里冰封，万里雪飘。望长城内外，唯余莽莽，大河上下，顿失滔滔。山舞银蛇，原驰蜡象，欲与天公试比高。须晴日，看红装素裹，分外妖娆。

江山如此多娇，引无数英雄竞折腰。惜秦皇汉武，略输文采；唐宗宋祖，稍逊风骚。一代天骄，成吉思汗，只识弯弓射大雕。俱往矣，数风流人物，还看今朝。

(in regular script)   (in cursive hand)

Note: poem by *Mao Zedong*.

Writing in the seal script requires strokes to be smooth and curved, and the structural form to be delicate and elegant.

Example 4.7 writing vertically (from right to left), in the seal script and regular script, respectively:

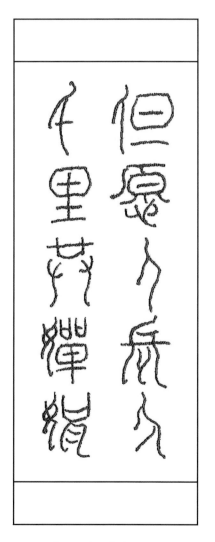 

(in seal script)   (in regular script)

Note: famous quotation from a poem by *Su Shi*.

Calligraphy in the seal script is often looked upon as a picture. Sometimes, artists use the seal script to draw and write in a 'composition style'. From a distance and at a glance, the writing illustrates a picture; but when looked at closely, a beautiful piece of calligraphy is presented.

Example 4.8 writing in the seal script and 'composition style':

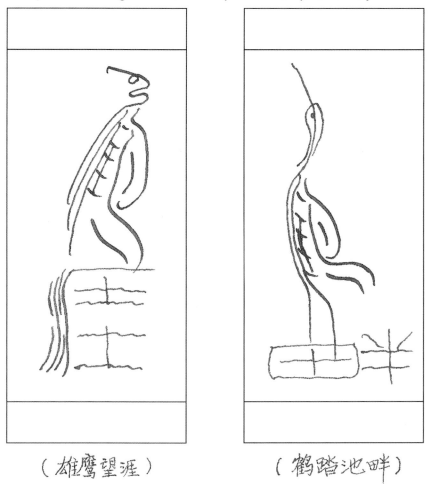

（ 雄鹰望涯 ）　　　（ 鹤踏池畔 ）

Note: the writing on the left is for the four-character phrase 雄鹰望涯, which means 'a handsome eagle is watching over a cliff'; the writing on the right is another four-character phrase 鹤踏池畔, which means 'a beautiful crane is treading on a pond bank'.

Chinese Characters in Use Today

当今实用汉字

5

"I'm very anxious not to fall into archaism or 'literary' diction. I want my vocabulary to have a very large range, but the words must be alive."

American novelist James R. Agee

It is indeed amazing that Chinese characters have survived for thousands of years. With China's rapid and continuous economic and social development since the end of the 1970s,[†] Mandarin Chinese and simplified Chinese characters are becoming increasingly popular. However, to non-Chinese speakers, the sheer number of *hanzi* is equally amazing and breathtaking, and they cannot help but ask the same question time and again: "How many *hanzi* do I need to recognize and understand to be able to read Chinese (newspapers and magazines) with confidence and speed?"

Unfortunately there is not a definitive answer to this question. However, as will be discussed later in this chapter and as a rough guide, **to be Chinese literate, non-Chinese speakers should aim to master some 1800 characters**.

[†] Chinese economic reform started from 1978.

5.1 Introduction

Broadly speaking, all the different scripts that represent different languages in the world can be categorized into three groups. The first group consists of phonemic characters, in which each character represents a phoneme. Languages that use phonemic characters include English, Greek, Russian and Arabic. The second group consists of syllabic characters, in which each character represents a syllable. Japanese uses syllabic characters. The third group consists of logographic characters, in which each character represents a morpheme. Nowadays Chinese is the only language in the world that uses logographic characters.

Logographic characters are not letters but, in most cases, meaningful entities. Of all the scripts currently in use in the world, *hanzi* represent a collection of characters that combine form, sound and meaning — albeit the sounds are not precisely embedded; all the other characters only combine form and sound, and meaning is associated with words rather than characters.

Given the fact that there are only 26 characters (letters) in the Latin alphabet, there is no doubt that the required 1800 characters that a non-Chinese speaker should aim to master seem a little daunting. However, it is very important to put this into perspective and appreciate that:
- Most Chinese characters are words themselves (single-character words, to be precise), so having mastered 1800 characters implies that one has already understood at least 1800 Chinese words.
- Amongst all Chinese words, single-character words and two-character words together command an absolute majority, see Table 5-3.
- Although one has a stiff learning curve in order to study *hanzi* at the beginning, taking in and absorbing (and making an educated guess at sometimes) hundreds of thousands of words will become progressively easier with practice and usage.
- Making up new words (of two or more characters) in Chinese is very flexible and powerful.

We shall now examine the quantitative feature of *hanzi* — the total number versus the number of characters in frequent use. We will also discuss the reasons behind the recommendation that non-Chinese speakers should aim to master some 1800 Chinese characters for confident and speedy reading. The last section of this chapter will introduce and explain in detail the 120 'basic and elementary' Chinese characters.

5.2 Growing Numbers of Chinese Characters

Hanzi, as a repository of the logographic characters used to record the Chinese language, have come a very long way and are the result of evolution over thousands of years. The origins and development of Chinese characters before oracle bone script (dated 1300BC) are still attracting lots of research and investigation from researchers in many different disciplines. However, from some 4000 characters of oracle bone script well over 3000 years ago, Chinese characters have been constantly growing and now have reached well beyond 50000 in total, albeit no one is sure of the precise total number.

The best way to trace the historic growth of *hanzi* is to examine all the known Chinese dictionaries of the past 2000 years. Table 5-1 lists some of the major dictionaries and the number of characters they have collected.

Dictionary	Author	Number of Characters	Time (AD) of Publication
Xunzuanpian [a]	*Yang Xiong*	5340	5 (*Han* dynasty)
Shuowen Jiezi	*Xu Shen*	9353	121 (*Han* dynasty)
Zilin	*Lü Chen*	12824	400 (Eastern *Jin*)
Yupian	*Gu Yewang*	16917	543 (Southern *Liang*)
Guangyun	*Chen Pengnian et al*	26194	1008 (*Song* dynasty)

Zihui	Mei Yingzuo	33179	1615 (*Ming* dynasty)
Kangxi Dictionary	Zhang Yushu et al	47035	1716 (*Qing* dynasty)
Great China Dictionary	Ouyang Pucun et al	48000	1915
Encyclopedia Dictionary of the Chinese Language	Zhang Qiyun et al	49880	1962 – 1968
Great Dictionary of Chinese Characters	Xu Zhongshu et al	56000	1986

[a] **Xunzuanpian** is not actually a dictionary but a text book for teaching Chinese characters

Table 5-1: Some Chinese dictionaries of the past 2000 years and the number of characters they have collected. All the dictionaries listed in the table are available in the National Library of China.[1]

To see if there is any pattern in the growth of *hanzi* over the last few thousand years, the data in Table 5-1 and the 4000 characters of oracle bone script (around 1300BC) are plotted in Figure 5.1. Examining the growth outline, a few things can be observed:

- The growth of *hanzi* from 1300BC to 5AD is very slow, roughly one more character per year on average.
- Since 5AD *hanzi* have constantly grown at a much faster rate — about 25 more characters per year on average.
- Although it is very difficult to see an overall growth pattern, it seems that the 'limited growth' [†] can be observed over some periods of time.
- From the time when **Zihui** was published to the time when **Kangxi Dictionary** was published, *hanzi* experienced a very steep growth path — approximately 14000 more characters in a century.

[†] Limited growth indicates a growth that can be modelled by logistic equation.[2]

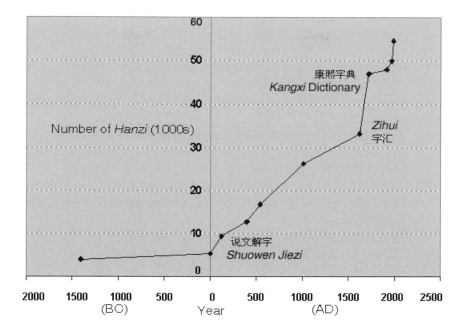

Figure 5.1: Growth of Chinese characters.

It is far beyond the scope of this book to explore and numerically analyse the growth outline shown in Figure 5.1. However, by applying some common sense, it is reasonable to argue that the fast expansion of *hanzi* since 5AD reflects the following facts in China over last 2000 years:

- increasing social and cultural activities
- increasing production (mainly agricultural) and trade activities
- scientific and technological advances
- increasing cultural and trade exchanges between China and other countries
- geopolitical changes and wars

5.3 Limited Number of *Hanzi* in Frequent Use

Like a coin, the quantitative feature of *hanzi* has two sides — one side shows the total number of Chinese characters and the other indicates the number of those characters in frequent use.

Compared with the staggering total number of more than 50000, the number of characters in frequent use is actually significantly smaller and is roughly stable during any specific period of time. The following books are a few typical examples to show the usage aspect of *hanzi*:

- **Confucian Analects** (completed around the beginning of the Warring States) contains 15883 characters, but uses only 1382 different ones.[3]
- **The Mencius** (completed during the latter half of the Warring States) contains 35402 characters, but uses only 1935 different ones.[4]
- The famous poets of the *Tang* dynasty *Li Bai* (701–762), *Du Fu* (712–770) and *Bai Juyi* (772–846) have used 3560, 4350 and 4600 different characters in their 994, 1500 and 3000 poems, respectively.[5]
- The renowned classical Chinese novel **A Dream of Red Mansions** (completed *c*. 1754) contains 731,017 characters, but only uses 4462 different characters.[6]
- The first 4 volumes of **The Selective Works of Mao Zedong** (completed 1921–1949) contain about 660 thousand characters, but only use 2981 different ones.[5]

5.3.1 Contemporary Chinese characters

In 1988, the China National Language and Character Working Committee published two milestone standard tables for contemporary Chinese: in that January, joined with the Ministry of Education, it published **Current Frequently Used Chinese Characters** (**Frequently Used Characters** for short) to be used in Chinese language teaching; in that March, joined with the General Administration of Press and Publication, it published **Current Commonly Used Chinese Characters** (**Commonly Used Characters** for short) to be used in press, publication and information prcessing.[7]

Frequently Used Characters include 2500 'most frequently used' characters (as listed in Appendix I for the convenience of readers and Chinese learners) and 1000 'next most frequently used' characters. Verifying against a sample of 2 million characters, the committee gained significant insight into the usage of contemporary Chinese characters, and it has been found that: 2500 'most frequently used characters' covered 97.97% of the sample; 1000 'next most frequently used characters' 1.51% — an insignificant increase; all together 3500 characters 99.48%.

Commonly Used Characters contain 7000 characters in total, including all the 3500 characters in **Frequently Used Characters**.

It can be readily seen from the above statistical result, by mastering the 2500 most frequently used characters, a Chinese speaker can achieve a reading recognition rate of 98% on average. That is to say, one might encounter about 20 unknown characters when reading an essay of 1000 characters, and about 100 unknown characters when reading an article of 5000 characters. However, given that the redundancy [†] of written Chinese on average is about 65%,[8] mastering 2500 most frequently used characters actually equips readers with a very high reading capacity.

5.3.2 To be Chinese literate

What is literacy? The basic definition of literacy is the ability to read and write. To be literate in a particular language, one has to be able to read and write in the language in question. Hence, for primary school pupils in any country, learning to read is always the first and main objective of the language curriculum.

The logographic feature of Chinese characters determines that mastering a certain number of *hanzi* is the prerequisite to reading and hence to being literate. For over 2000 years, there has actually always been a '*hanzi* threshold' of 1300 – 1800 characters as a target for teaching pupils at the very beginning of their education. In the last century, all the efforts for reducing the illiteracy rate in China have aimed to enable illiterates to recognize and understand a certain number of *hanzi*, see Table 5-4 for detail.

The question is now, for non-Chinese speakers to become Chinese

---

[†] Redundancy in a language is the use of duplicative, unnecessary or useless words. Claude Shannon has shown a 75% redundancy of English.[9]

literate and to be able to read Chinese with confidence and speed, how many Chinese characters should they aim to learn and master within a certain period of time? Compared with Chinese children and illiterates, non-Chinese speakers did not grow up in a Chinese environment, it is therefore natural that they are likely to need to know more *hanzi* to reach the similar level of reading capacity. Unfortunately, at present there is not a standard or commonly recognized '*hanzi* threshold' for non-Chinese speakers.

Ref	Time of Publication	Size of Sample	Number of Unique Characters	Usage Frequency (%)
I	1977	21,629,372	6335	1500 *hanzi*: **95.97**
				2000 *hanzi*: **98.14**
II	1986	11,873,029	7745	1500 *hanzi*: **94.76**
				2000 *hanzi*: **97.29**
III	1986	1,807,398	4574	1500 *hanzi*: **95.94**
				2000 *hanzi*: **98.06**

I: *Hanzi Frequency Table* (sample includes contemporary books, newspapers and magazines)
II: *Table of 3000 High Frequency Hanzi* (sample includes the academic papers during the period of 1977 – 1982)
III: *Hanzi Frequency Table* (sample includes a variety of language materials)

Table 5-2: Some statistical results on contemporary Chinese characters.[10]

To give Chinese learners a reasonable target to aim for, and to encourage more studies to address the issue, **a '*hanzi* threshold' of 1800 characters for non-Chinese speakers is therefore recommended**. This recommendation is mainly based on the following factors:

1) In contemporary Chinese, 1800 characters have covered a usage frequency of more than 95%, see Table 5-2.
2) 1800 is the upper limit of all the data in Table 5-4.
3) The redundancy of written Chinese is 65% on average.

Reference	Summary of Survey and Result
Frequency Dictionary of Current Frequently Used Chinese Vocabularies [11]	Sample: 25m characters in total, 100,000 different words. Result: the dictionary includes the most popular 10,000 words, in which single-character words take 57.53%, two-character words 39.25%.
Statistics and Analysis of Frequently Used and Vocabulary Forming Chinese Characters [12]	Sample: all the vocabulary entries, from three vocabulary dictionaries, that only contain characters within the 3500 'frequently used characters'. Result: 70343 vocabulary entries in total, which include 4555 single-character words, 496,415 two-character words, 8308 three-character words, 6922 four-character words, 702 five-character words, and 215 six-character words.
Statistics and Analysis of Chinese Vocabularies [13]	Sample: all the words from the unified Chinese language textbooks for the 10-year primary and second education system. Result: 520,934 characters in total, 18177 different words, and average word length is 1.98 characters.

Table 5-3: Some statistical results on Chinese vocabulary in contemporary Chinese.

Furthermore, **a time frame of 18 months is suggested for learners to reach the recommended target of mastering 1800 characters**. The main considerations for this include:

1) As shown in Table 5-4, pupils in Chinese schools are required to be able to recognize up to 1800 characters by the end of their first two years of schooling. Given that Chinese schools normally have a 3-month holiday break each year, pupils in Chinese schools are actually learning some 100 characters per month on average within their first two years of education.

2) Setting oneself the same goal of learning 100 characters a month, mastering 1800 characters naturally requires a time frame of 18 months. If one can manage 20 days in a month to spend some time studying Chinese, then 100 characters a month will be translated into 5 characters per study day.

This sounds very reasonable.

3) As it is well known, foreign language study is a long term commitment, and the language proficiency and accumulation of vocabularies come with time and experience. However it is also well recognized that the best and most effective approach is to do it in concentration and to reach a certain level very quickly at the beginning. This is even more important with the study of Chinese characters.

Time	Teaching Recipients	Textbook/Reference	Hanzi Threshold
1st century BC – 7th century AD	children at the beginning of their formal education	*Jijiupian*	1649
13th century – the beginning of 20th century	children at the beginning of their formal education	a) *Three Character Classic* b) *Hundred Family Names* c) *Thousand Character Classic*	1476
1925	illiterates within urban inhabitants	*Thousand Characters for Civilians*	1368
1946	illiterates within peasants	*Characters Needed by Masses*	1440
1952	illiterates or semi-illiterates	*Frequently Used Characters*	1500 （1st set and 2nd set of frequently used characters）
1956	pupils of year 1 and year 2 in primary schools	*Primary School Chinese Language Syllabus (Draft)*	to be able to recognize up to 1500 characters
1988	illiterates or semi-illiterates	*Literacy Work Regulations*	target for peasants: 1500 characters

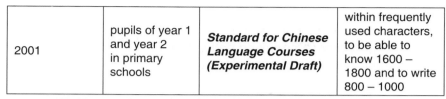

| 2001 | pupils of year 1 and year 2 in primary schools | *Standard for Chinese Language Courses (Experimental Draft)* | within frequently used characters, to be able to know 1600 – 1800 and to write 800 – 1000 |

Table 5-4: The *hanzi* threshold of the Chinese language study in the last 21 centuries.[14]

5.4 The 120 Basic and Elementary Chinese Characters

Although compiling a full list of 1800 characters for non-Chinese speakers is beyond the scope of this book, to jump start the beginners' journey of learning Chinese, an innovative list of 120 'basic and elementary' Chinese characters is proposed in this section. There are many benefits to fully understanding these 120 characters:

1) It enables the essence of Chinese characters and their formation to be registered in one's mind quickly and firmly.
2) It will help learners grasp many basic and most popular radicals, which will greatly benefit further study.
3) It enables learners to become used to Chinese pronunciation and tones quickly.
4) Some very basic and useful sentences can be constructed from the characters in the list.

Where does this list come from? The majority of the characters in the list actually come from a survey carried out during the course of writing this book. Participants of the survey include the following groups of people:

1) those who grew up in China but have been living and working in English (or other languages) speaking countries for more than 10 years
[This is the largest group.]
2) the teenagers from the families with parents from the above group
[For these teenage boys and girls, their social and school environments are not Chinese, but at home they talk with their families in a mix of Chinese and the local languages. They study Chinese from their parents at home and/or from

going to weekend Chinese schools.]
3) adults and school children from China
4) some Chinese-speaking native English speakers
5) some people from Hong Kong

What they were asked to do was very simple: to write down quickly (in 10 – 20 minutes) a list of 100 Chinese characters which they personally think are most basic and elementary, and which come to their minds immediately. The end results overlapped surprisingly well, and almost all the characters that appeared in more than 80% of replies have been included in the list of 120 basic and elementary characters.

The rest of the 120 characters are selected by comprising, as well as possible, the following criteria:
1) To reflect humanity's most basic understanding of nature and themselves;
2) To be single-component characters;
3) To be essential in constructing Chinese sentences;
4) To appear in some of the most popular daily greetings.

5.4.1 List of 120 characters

It should be noted that, within all the tables in this section:
a) In the title rows, 'RA' means radical, 'SC' stroke count, 'PY' *pinyin*.
b) The order of the characters means nothing but is used merely for convenience of reference; see the next section for some examples of their usage.
c) In the *'Hanzi'* column, all those within round brackets — 10 in total — are the short forms of their corresponding characters, they can only be used as character components (to construct characters) and can also be radicals (see Chapter 6 for detail on radical).
d) Out of the 120 characters, as appeared in the shaded cells in the *'Hanzi'* column, 50 can be used as radicals. Together with the 10 short forms, this list of 120 'basic and elementary' Chinese characters has included 60 radicals.
e) Only 25 characters use the radicals, as in the shaded cells in the 'RA' column, that are beyond the scope of the list.

Group 1: **Numerals**

No	*Hanzi*	RA†	SC‡	PY§	Meaning
1	一	一	1	*yī*	one; a, an
2	二	二	2	*èr*	two
3	三	一	3	*sān*	three
4	四	口	5	*sì*	four
5	五	二	4	*wǔ*	five
6	六	八	4	*liù*	six
7	七	一	2	*qī*	seven
8	八 (ソ)	八	2	*bā*	eight
9	九	丿	2	*jiǔ*	nine
10	十	十	2	*shí*	ten
11	百	白	6	*bǎi*	hundred; numerous
12	千	十	3	*qiān*	thousand; many
13	万	一	3	*wàn*	ten thousand; innumerable

† Radical; ‡ Stroke Count; § *Pinyin*

Group 2: **Animals**

No	*Hanzi*	RA	SC	PY	Meaning
14	鸟	鸟	5	*niǎo*	bird
15	鱼	鱼	8	*yú*	fish
16	马	马	3	*mǎ*	horse
17	牛	牛	4	*niú*	ox, cow, bull
18	羊	羊	6	*yáng*	sheep, goat
19	狗	犭	8	*gǒu*	dog
20	猫	犭	11	*māo*	cat
21	虫	虫	6	*chóng*	insects; worms

Group 3: **Natural Phenomena and Objects**

No	*Hanzi*	RA	SC	PY	Meaning
22	日	日	4	*rì*	sun; day, daytime
23	月	月	4	*yuè*	moon; month
24	光	儿	6	*guāng*	light, shine
25	天	大	4	*tiān*	sky; day; weather; heaven
26	气	气	4	*qì*	gas, steam
27	云	二	4	*yún*	cloud; say
28	雨	雨	8	*yǔ*	rain
29	风	风	4	*fēng*	wind
30	金 (钅)	金	8	*jīn*	gold, metal; money
31	木	木	4	*mù*	tree, timber, wood
32	水 (氵)	水	4	*shuǐ*	water
33	火 (灬)	火	4	*huǒ*	fire

34	土	土	3	*tǔ*	soil, earth
35	山	山	3	*shān*	mountain, hill
36	石	石	5	*shí*	stone, rock
37	草	艹	9	*cǎo*	grass; hasty

Group 4: Human — Inventions

No	Hanzi	RA	SC	PY	Meaning
38	刀 (刂)	刀	2	*dāo*	knife
39	车	车	4	*chē*	cart, vehicle
40	门	门	3	*mén*	door, gate
41	衣 (衤)	衣	6	*yī*	clothes
42	饭	饣	7	*fàn*	cooked rice, meal, food

Group 5: Human — Body, Activities and Relationships

No	Hanzi	RA	SC	PY	Meaning
43	人 (亻)	人	2	*rén*	human, people, person
44	头	大	5	*tóu*	head; top, first; chief, boss
45	口	口	3	*kǒu*	mouth; entrance
46	耳	耳	6	*ěr*	ear
47	手 (扌)	手	4	*shǒu*	hand
48	足	足	7	*zú*	foot; enough; satisfy
49	心 (忄)	心	4	*xīn*	heart; mind; centre
50	皮	皮	5	*pí*	skin; outer
51	目	目	5	*mù*	eye
52	父	父	4	*fù*	father
53	母	母	5	*mǔ*	mother; female
54	夫	大	4	*fū*	man; husband
55	子	子	3	*zǐ*	child; offspring; seed
56	儿	儿	2	*ér*	child; son; young man
57	女	女	3	*nǚ*	girl; woman
58	男	田	7	*nán*	man, male
59	士	士	3	*shì*	gentleman; scholar; solider
60	生	生	5	*shēng*	birth; life, living
61	老	耂	6	*lǎo*	old; aged
62	吃	口	6	*chī*	eat
63	喝	口	12	*hē*	drink
64	听	口	7	*tīng*	hear, listen to; obey
65	说	讠	9	*shuō*	speak, say, talk
66	看	目	9	*kàn*	see, look
67	见	见	4	*jiàn*	see; meet with
68	言 (讠)	言	7	*yán*	words, speech; say
69	走	走	7	*zǒu*	walk, go

70	问	门	6	wèn	ask, inquire
71	请	讠	10	qǐng	invite; ask, request
72	谢	讠	12	xiè	thank; decline
73	你	亻	7	nǐ	you
74	我	戈	7	wǒ	I, me
75	他	亻	5	tā	he, him
76	她	女	6	tā	she, her
77	它	宀	5	tā	it

Group 6: Human — Sense and Abstraction

No	*Hanzi*	RA	SC	PY	Meaning
78	上	一	3	shàng	top; go up
79	下	一	3	xià	below, under; get down
80	左	工	5	zuǒ	left
81	右	口	5	yòu	right
82	前	刂	9	qián	front; former
83	后	口	6	hòu	back; after; behind
84	内	门	4	nèi	inside, internal; within
85	外	夕	5	wài	outside, external; foreign
86	中	丨	4	zhōng	centre, middle
87	大	大	3	dà	big, large
88	小	小	3	xiǎo	small, little
89	多	夕	6	duō	many, much
90	少	小	4	shǎo	few, less
91	黑	黑	12	hēi	black; dark
92	白	白	5	bái	white; pure
93	红	纟	6	hóng	red
94	绿	纟	11	lǜ	green
95	好	女	6	hǎo	good, fine
96	力	力	2	lì	force; capability; power
97	早	日	6	zǎo	morning; early; soon
98	晚	日	11	wǎn	evening, night; late
99	先	儿	6	xiān	advance; first; ancestor
100	年	干	6	nián	year, annual
101	东	一	5	dōng	east
102	西	覀	6	xī	west
103	南	十	9	nán	south
104	北	匕	5	běi	north
105	春	日	9	chūn	spring
106	夏	夂	10	xià	summer
107	秋	禾	9	qiū	autumn, fall
108	冬	夂	5	dōng	winter

Group 7: Some Essential Characters in Constructing Chinese Phases and Sentences

No	Hanzi	RA†	SC‡	PY§	Meaning
109	的	白	8	de	of; possessive
110	在	土	6	zài	at, in, on; exist
111	是	日	9	shì	be; yes, indeed
112	个	人	3	gè	piece; single; entries
113	有	月	6	yǒu	have, possess, own
114	了	一	2	le	(grammatical) particle of completed action — normally used after a (grammatical) verb/adjective
				liǎo	understand; end, finish
115	不	一	4	bù	no, not
116	和	口	8	hé	and; harmony; peace; sum
117	太	大	4	tài	very, extremely, over
118	再	冂	6	zài	twice; again
109	这	辶	7	zhè	this, here, the
120	们	亻	5	mén	(grammatical) adjunct pronoun indicating plural

† Radical; ‡ Stroke Count; § Pinyin

5.4.2 Examples of using the basic and elementary characters

Please note that, in the following examples, the numbers within square brackets (e.g. [117, 95, 114]) are the character order numbers in the list provided in the previous section.

先生 [99, 60] — gentleman
女士 [57, 59] — lady
夫人 [54, 43] — Madame, wife
太太 [117, 117] — wife, Madame
父母 [52, 53] — parents
儿子 [56, 55] — son
女儿 [57, 56] — daughter

谢谢 [72, 72] — thank you, thanks
再见 [118, 67] — good bye, see you
早上好 [97, 78, 95] — good morning
晚上好 [98, 78, 95] — good evening
太好了 [117, 95, 114] — wonderful, excellent

早饭 [97, 42] — breakfast
中饭 [86, 42] — lunch
晚饭 [98, 42] — dinner
吃饭 [62, 42] — dine

天气 [25, 26] — weather
下雨了。 [79, 28, 114] — It's raining.

风光 [29, 24] — scene, sight
火山 [33, 35] — volcano

八百万 [8, 11, 13] — 8 million

大年三十 [87, 100, 3, 10] — Chinese New Year's Eve

我看见他们了。 [74, 66, 67, 75, 120, 114] — I see (saw) them.

她听见了。 [76, 64, 67, 114] — She hears (heard) that.

请听她说。 [71, 64, 76, 65] — Please listen to her.

这不是我的。 [119, 115, 111, 74, 109] — This is not mine.

请问,他在不在? [71, 70, 75, 110, 115, 110] — Excuse me, is he in?

Looking up Characters in a Dictionary

6

查字典技巧

"The trouble with the dictionary is that you have to know how a word is spelled before you can look it up to see how it is spelled."

Will Cuppy

A dictionary is the most basic reference tool we use during our literate lives.

When learning a foreign language, a foreign dictionary is a 'life jacket'. For example, if an English speaker decides to take up the challenge of learning Chinese, a Chinese-English dictionary will initially be indispensable, and gradually a Chinese dictionary and an English-Chinese dictionary will also come in very handy with the progress of language study. However, unlike using an English dictionary (from which an unknown word can be easily located by following the alphabetic order of the word in question), when it comes to using a Chinese-English or Chinese dictionary, the users need a fairly good grasp of the structure of *hanzi*. More importantly, they need to understand the concept of Chinese indexing components, often referred to as radicals, to be able to look for any unknown Chinese characters.

It is highly recommended that, for the best effect, this chapter should be read in conjunction with a Chinese-English or Chinese dictionary at hand.

Figure 6.1: Locating the character '计' by means of its *pinyin 'ji'*.

14

部首查字表

    1. 这个查字表用的部首跟一般字典的部首基本相同，表内有部首189个。

    2. 部首次序按部首的笔画数目排列，同画数的按起笔（书写时的第一笔）的笔形横（一）竖（丨）撇（丿）点（丶）折（乙，包括一丁乚等笔形）顺序排列。

    3. 难查的字分收在几个部首里。如"寺"在土部，也在寸部；"命"在口部，也在人部等。分不清部首的字，按起笔的笔形，收入一、丨、丿、丶、乙五个单笔部首里。如"井、甘、再"收入一部。还有《难查字笔画索引》备查。

    4. 碰到不认识的字，用部首查字法查。查字的时候，先在《部首目录》里找到这个字的部首页码，按页码从查字表里找到这个部首，再把要查的字除去部首，按笔画数和起笔笔形查找。如查不到，定是搞错部首，可在另一个部首里找，或者按起笔笔形的部首里查找。如还是查不到，再在《难查字笔画索引》里查找。

（一）　部首目录（附部首名称）

    1. 下面的顺序是：部首，部首名称，查字表的页码。2. 括号里是变形部首和名称。3. 部首名称是参考小学语文课本等材料拟订的。4. 部首名称里的"二、卜、八、人"等字，或用于"头"，或用于"底"，或用于"旁"，如"二"的"云、些"，"卜"的"占、卜、卧"等，它的名称可以按它所在的部位称"二字头"、"二字底"、"卜字旁"等，这些部首的名称不一一标出。

一画		二画		（卜）		夕 见刀	
一 横	17	二 二	19	冂 同字框	20	几 几	22
丨 竖	17	十 十	19	亻 单人旁	20	（几）	
丿 撇	18	厂 厂字旁	19	八 八	21	几 几	22
丶 点	18	匚 三框	19	（丷）		亠 文字头	22
乙 折	18	刂 立刀旁	19	人 人	21	冫 两点水	22
（一丁乚）		卜 卜	20	（入）		冖 秃宝盖	23
				勹 包字头	22	讠 言字旁	23

Figure 6.2 (a): The table of 189 radicals — 1/3.

15

（言）			夂	折文	34	犬	犬	43	殳	殳	48

（言）　　　　　　夂 折文 34　　犬 犬 43　　殳 殳 48
卩 单耳旁 23　　饣 食字旁 34　　歹 歹 43　　文 文 48
（巳）　　　　　　（食）　　　　　车 车 44　　方 方 48
阝 左耳旁 23　　广 广字旁 34　　（车：车字旁）　火 火 48
阝 右耳旁 24　　忄 竖心旁 34　　（車）　　　（灬：火字旁）
凵 凶字框 24　　（卜）　　　　　戈 戈 44
刀 刀 24　　　　门 门 35　　　比 比 44　　斗 斗字旁 49
（⺈）　　　　　　（門）　　　　　瓦 瓦 44　　灬 四点底 49
力 力 25　　　　氵 三点水 35　　止 止 44　　户 户字头 49
厶 厶 25　　　　宀 宝盖 37　　　支 敲字旁 44　礻 示字旁 49
又 又 25　　　　辶 走之 38　　　卜 见忄 　　心 心 49
（又）　　　　　　彐 寻字头 38　　日 日 44　　聿 聿 50
廴 建字旁 25　　（彐彑）　　　　曰 曰 45　　（聿聿）
巳 见卩 25　　　尸 尸字头 39　　（日）　　　爿 爿字旁 50
　　　　　　　　己 己 39　　　水 水 45　　毋 毋 50
三画　　　　（巳）　　　　　（水）　　　（母）
工 工 25　　　　弓 弓 39　　　贝 贝 45
土 土 25　　　　子 子 39　　　（貝）　　　**五画**
（扌：提土旁）　（孑）　　　　　见 见 46
士 士 26　　　　屮 出字头 39　　（見）　　　示 示字底 50
扌 提手旁 26　　（屮）　　　　　牛 牛 46　　石 石 50
艹 草字头 28　　女 女 39　　　（牜：牛字旁）（石：石字旁）
寸 寸 29　　　　（女：女字旁）　（⺧：牛字头）龙 龙 51
廾 开字底 30　　纟 绞丝旁 40　　手 手 46　　（龍）
大 大 30　　　　（糸）　　　　　毛 毛 46　　业 业 51
尢 尤 30　　　　马 马 41　　　气 气 46　　氺 见水
弋 弋 30　　　　（馬）　　　　　攵 反文旁 46　目 目 51
小 小 30　　　　幺 幼字旁 41　　片 片字旁 47　（目：目字旁）
（⺌）　　　　　巛 三拐 41　　　斤 斤 47　　田 田 51
口 口字旁 30　　　　　　　　　爪 爪 47　　罒 四字头 51
囗 方框儿 32　　**四画**　　　（爫：爪字头）皿 皿字底 52
巾 巾 32　　　　王 王 41　　　父 父字头 47　钅 金字旁 52
山 山 32　　　　（⺩：王字旁）　月 月字旁 47　（金）
彳 双人旁 33　　韦 韦 42　　　（月）　　　矢 矢字旁 53
彡 三撇 33　　　（韋）　　　　　欠 欠字旁 48　禾 禾 53
犭 反犬旁 33　　木 木 42　　　风 风 48　　（禾：禾木旁）
夕 夕 34　　　　（木：木字旁）　（鳳）　　　白 白 53

Figure 6.2 (b): The table of 189 radicals — 2/3.

16

瓜 瓜字旁 54	血 血字旁 58	谷 谷字旁 61	韋 见韦
用 用 54	舟 舟字旁 58	豸 豸字旁 61	**十画**
鸟 鸟 54	衣 衣 58	角 角字旁 61	門 門字框 63
（鳥）	羊 羊 58	言 言 61	髟 髟字头 63
疒 病字旁 54	（芉羊）	（言：见讠）	馬 见马
立 立 55	米 米 59	辛 辛字旁 61	**十一画**
穴 穴宝盖 55	（米：米字旁）		麥 见麦
衤 衣字旁 55	聿 见聿	**八画**	鹵 见卤
聿 见聿	艮 艮 59	青 青字旁 61	鳥 见鸟
艮 见艮	（艮：艮字旁）	其 其 61	魚 见鱼
疋 疋 55	羽 羽 59	雨 雨字头 61	麻 麻 63
（正）	糸 系 59	（⻗）	鹿 鹿 63
皮 皮字旁 55	（糸见纟）	齿 齿字旁 61	**十二画**
矛 矛 55		（齒）	黽 见黾
母 见毋	**七画**	黾 黾 61	黑 黑 63
	麦 麦字旁 59	（黽）	**十三画**
六画	（麥）	佳 佳 61	鼠 鼠字旁 63
来 来字旁 55	走 走字旁 59	金 金 62	**十四画**
老 老 56	赤 赤字旁 59	（金：见钅）	鼻 鼻字旁 63
耳 耳 56	車 见车	食 见饣	**十五画**
臣 臣字旁 56	豆 豆 59	鱼 鱼 62	齒 见齿
西 西 56	酉 酉字旁 60	（魚）	**十七画**
（西：西字头）	辰 辰 60	門 见门	龍 见龙
页 页字旁 56	豕 豕 60		
（頁）	卤 卤字旁 60	**九画**	
虍 虎字头 56	（鹵）	革 革字旁 62	
虫 虫 56	里 里 60	頁 见页	
缶 缶 57	贝 见贝	骨 骨字旁 62	
舌 舌字旁 57	見 见见	鬼 鬼字旁 62	
竹 竹 57	足 足 60	食 食 62	
（⺮：竹字头）	（⻊：足字旁）	（食：见饣）	
臼 臼 58	身 身字旁 61	風 见风	
自 自 58	釆 釆 61	音 音 62	

Figure 6.2(c): The table of 189 radicals — 3/3.

（二）查 字 表

字右边的号码指字典正文的页码。有"〔 〕"的是繁体或异体字。

一部

一 429

一画
丁 74
七 281

二画
三 313
干 105
于 443
亏 498
上 321
寸 56
才 29
下 397
丈 463
兀 391
万 378
与 445

三画
丰 96
开 189
井 179
天 363
夫 99
无 389
韦 381
专 482
丐 104
丏 519
廿 521
五 390

卅 529
不 26
尤 441
友 442
丑 47
牙 419
屯 374
互 140

四画
未 383
末 251
击 152
正 469
甘 105
世 333
业 428
本 16
可 193
且 294
冊 539
〔册〕 32
册 32
丙 23
丕 524
丘 298
左 491
右 443
布 27
平 276
东 76
丛 54
丝 345

五画
再 455
吏 212
亘 504
亚 419
考 191
老 206
共 114
在 455
存 56
百 8
而 86
有 442
死 345
〔亙〕 504
夹 160
至 473
尧 426
夷 430
成 41
戌 412
戍 339
戎 309
丞 497

六画
求 299
严 421
〔听〕 352
甫 101
更 111
束 340
丽 212

两 216
巫 388
〔夾〕 160
来 203

七画
忝 534
武 391
表 21
奉 98
〔長〕 37
〔東〕 76
事 334
枣 456
其 283
〔亞〕 419
画 143
〔兩〕 216
〔面〕 246
〔來〕 203
〔並〕 23
巹 509

八画
奏 489
毒 78
巷 403
韭 181
甚 325
柬 164
歪 376
甭 494
面 246

九画

艳 423
泰 356
秦 295
恭 113
髙 504
爕 547
哥 109
奭 521
夏 397

十至
十一画
焉 420
堇 511
爽 342
〔棗〕 456
棘 156
〔甦〕 348
〔畫〕 143

十二至
十四画
赖 203
〔夏〕 441
〔爾〕 87
暨 509
颐 549

十五
画以上
嚚 86
整 469
臻 467
〔蠚〕 210
龚 257

矗 500

丨部

一至二画
卜 25
上 321
也 427

三画
丰 96
韦 381
中 475
内 258
〔弔〕 73
书 337

四画
北 14
卡 286
旧 182
归 122
半 10
史 331
央 423
冉 305
且 294
由 441
申 325
甲 160
电 72
出 48
凹 4
凸 371

五至六画

Figure 6.3 (a): The index table of characters — the beginning page.

㉓

凛 220	记 157	诗 329	诸 480	谙 406	谵 289
〔凛〕220	**四画**	诘 171	读 79	**十画**	〔譟〕457
㲀 262	讲 167	〔誇〕198	谏 553	〔謹〕142	〔譯〕433
冖部	讵 512	诙 147	诼 552	〔講〕167	谴 549
二至四画	讳 148	诚 42	课 194	谟 520	〔議〕432
冗 310	讴 523	诠 528	诽 93	谠 500	**十五画**
写 406	讶 419	诛 479	〔論〕231	谡 532	**以上**
军 188	讷 521	话 143	诿 383	谣 426	〔讀〕79
农 263	讼 348	诞 63	谁 324	谢 406	〔讅〕423
五画以上	论 231	诟 505	谀 547	〔謡〕478	〔讑〕306
罕 129	讻 541	诡 124	调 365	谤 11	谶 497
冠 120	许 413	询 417	谄 36	谥 519	〔讒〕35
冢 551	讹 85	〔誡〕541	谅 433	谧 531	〔讓〕455
冥 249	讽 98	诤 550	译 532	谦 288	〔讙〕500
冤 448	设 323	诧 34	谆 485	**十一画**	〔讚〕543
幂 245	访 92	该 104	谅 217	谨 175	
〔幂〕245	诀 187	详 401	谈 356	〔謳〕523	**卩(巳)部**
	五画	诨 509	**九画**	谩 237	**一至四画**
讠(言)部	评 276	诮 433	谍 147	谪 550	卫 384
二画	证 469	诩 541	谐 497	谫 510	叩 196
计 157	诂 505	**七画**	谋 252	谬 250	卮 550
订 75	识 329	诚 174	谏 74	**十二画**	印 436
讣 101	诅 490	语 445	谏 164	谭 357	卯 239
认 308	诊 467	〔誌〕473	谒 429	谮 549	危 381
讥 152	诈 459	诬 388	谓 384	谯 527	**五画**
三画	诉 348	诮 293	谔 502	〔譅〕85	却 303
讦 511	诋 69	误 391	谖 542	〔識〕329	卵 230
讧 137	诌 478	诰 504	谕 548	谰 204	即 155
讨 360	〔註〕481	诱 443	〔諡〕531	谱 280	**六画以上**
让 306	〔詠〕439	诲 148	谗 35	〔譔〕483	卷 186
讯 417	译 433	诳 514	谛 71	〔譅〕469	卺 511
讪 530	词 53	说 344	谝 493	谲 512	〔卻〕303
议 432	诏 550	诵 348	谚 423	〔譏〕152	卸 407
讫 286	诒 544	〔認〕308	〔謅〕487	**十三至**	卿 297
〔託〕374	**六画**	**八画**	谜 244	**十四画**	
讯 417	诓 514	请 297	〔譚〕148	谳 543	**阝部**
	试 332	诸 264		〔護〕140	**(在左)**

Figure 6.3 (b): The index table of characters — the page on
which '计' is indexed.

6.1 An Example — Looking up the Character 计 (count; idea)

In this example, we shall refer exclusively to ***The Newly Compiled Elementary Student Dictionary*** [1] when we indicate specific pages.

Presuming you know this character and know it is pronounced in *pinyin* as *'ji'* with the 4th sound tone (refer to Chapter 2 — **Pronunciation of *Hanzi*)**, then looking it up in the main body of the dictionary is simple. Similar to English words in an English dictionary, Chinese characters in a Chinese dictionary appear in alphabetic order according to their *pinyin*. Therefore you can just flip to the section of characters beginning with *'j'*. Then, just as when using an English dictionary, you will have to examine the second letter in the *pinyin* of *'ji'* — *'i'* — and you will find there are many characters with this *pinyin* from page 152 to the middle of page 159. As all the characters with *pinyin 'ji'* are ordered from the 1st sound to the 4th sound, you should be able to locate character '计' easily on page 157, see Figure 6.1.

If, unfortunately, you do not know this character and there is no one you could ask for immediate help, how would you be able to find this character 计 in a Chinese dictionary? It is certainly not an exaggeration to say that this would be a difficult job if you have never used a Chinese dictionary before and do not know the necessary rules. Perhaps the first thought that comes into your mind would be to work out the 'stroke count' (the number of strokes, and in this case, 计 has 4 strokes). However, here, knowing the stroke count does not help at all. Firstly, Chinese characters in a Chinese dictionary are not ordered according to the stroke counts of characters (they are ordered alphabetically according to their *pinyin*); secondly, there is no index that maps stroke counts directly to characters (except, in most Chinese dictionaries, for a few hundred characters which are deemed to be very difficult to locate). So what do you do?

Recalling what has been discussed in Chapter 3 — **The Structure of Chinese Characters**, we understand that Chinese characters consist of components. Understanding these character components and the rules of disassembling Chinese characters into components is actually the key to looking up a Chinese character in a dictionary. Simply put for this example, the character 计 can be disassembled into two components '讠' and '十', in which '讠' is the indexing component and has 2 strokes. Within the list of 189 indexing components from page 14 to page 16 of the dictionary (see Figure 6.2), it can be found that '讠' is followed by number 23, which means all the characters with the indexing component '讠' are listed together beginning from page 23 in the index table of characters. Flipping to page 23 (see Figure 6.3(b)), you can find 计 is followed by number 157 which indicates that character 计 is defined and explained in detail on page 157 of the main body of the dictionary.

As can be seen, both approaches, of course, guide us to the same page — page 157 — for the character 计, but they are completely different and serve different purposes. The first is similar to using an English dictionary: it can only be used to look up a character that one can pronounce and spell in *pinyin*; the second can be used to look up any given character, even if one does not know the character in question.

6.2 Radical Indexing

Radical indexing nowadays is the de facto method for locating Chinese characters in a Chinese dictionary.

From the previous example, it can be seen that in order to look for an unknown character in a Chinese dictionary, two things are important: firstly, to learn the rules of disassembling Chinese characters into components; secondly, to understand the concept of 'indexing components' which are often referred to as 'radicals'. By introducing this unique concept of radicals (indexing components), the Chinese have developed a very efficient character locating method: 'radical indexing'.

Radical indexing actually adopts a 'divide and conquer' approach. Basically, as shown in the previous example, this method involves two steps:
1. Disassemble a character into components, and then identify its radical;

2. Locate the character in question among all the characters with the same radical.

This method is the result of an excellent balance between the two competing goals: ease of use and efficiency. As mentioned in Chapter 1, out of all Chinese characters, pictophonetic characters — which consist of semantic parts and phonetic parts — have a proportion of some 80%, and all these pictophonetic characters can be disassembled naturally into at least two components (and indeed, in most cases, only two components). Therefore, advantages of adopting this method are obvious.

Although there are a few hundred components within Chinese characters (refer to Chapter 3), a subset of these components is sufficient to act as indexing components (radicals) for locating Chinese characters in a dictionary by means of radical indexing. As a matter of fact, the definition of radicals is not universally conformed to a single standard among different dictionaries. For instance, **A Chinese-English Dictionary** [2] uses 226 radicals; in both **The Newly Compiled Elementary Student Dictionary** and **Xinhua Dictionary**,[3] there are 189 radicals; and **Kangxi Dictionary** [4] contains 214 radicals. It should be noted that nearly half of these 200 or so radicals are characters themselves.

6.3 Locating a Character by Means of Radical Indexing

Before listing the detailed steps to locate a Chinese character in a Chinese dictionary, let's firstly have a look at some basic features of a typical Chinese dictionary:

   a) In the main body of the dictionary, all the characters appear in alphabetic order according to their *pinyin*.
   b) Before the main body of the dictionary, there is a table for radical indexing, which consists of two lists — a list of radicals and a list of characters grouped according to their radicals.
   c) The first list — list of radicals — is comparatively small and contains all the radicals in ascending order of their stroke counts. Each radical is followed by a number indicating where the group of those characters corresponding to this particular radical starts in the list of characters.

d) The second list — list of characters — is comparatively large and includes all the characters contained in the dictionary. In this list, all the characters are grouped according to their radicals; all the groups are presented in the same order in which all the corresponding radicals appear in the list of radicals. Within each group, the characters are listed in ascending order of their stroke counts, and each character is followed by its page number in the main body of the dictionary.

So, in order to locate a Chinese character in a Chinese dictionary, the following steps are needed (recapping the example of looking up the character 计):

1) Disassemble a character into its basic components (计: 讠, 十);

2) Identify the radical, and work out the stroke count of this radical (讠 : 2);

3) Locate this radical in the list of radicals by the stroke count, and obtain the location of the group of characters with that particular radical (page 23);

4) Go to the location in the list of characters (page 23), work out the stroke count of the remainder of the character in question (十: 2), and via this second stroke count, find this character in the list and obtain the page number in the main body where this character is defined and explained in detail (page 157).

Initially, it may seem that using a Chinese dictionary is not an easy task. However, once the majority of the 200 or so radicals and the basic rules of disassembling Chinese characters are mastered, it is actually very easy and fun to use a Chinese dictionary.

6.4 Some Useful Tips

As can be seen from all the previous discussions in this chapter, to correctly identify the radical (indexing component) of an unknown character is the key to quickly looking it up in a (Chinese) dictionary. To this end, you may find the tips in this section very handy.

Component Disassembly of Some Special Chinese Characters

The following 4 tips are based on some of the 'Component Disassembly Rules' stipulated by ***Modern Chinese Common Character Component Standard of Elementary Teaching***.[5]

1. If a character possesses an inter-crossed structure, do not disassemble it.
Example 1: 串
Do not disassemble it into '中' and '中'.
To locate it in a dictionary, use its very first stroke (a very short perpendicular dash in the top-left corner, but regardless of the size, it is a perpendicular dash), ' 丨 ', as the indexing component and, by taking away that indexing component, the stroke count of the remainder should be 6.
Example 2: 东
Do not disassemble it into '七' and '小'.
To locate this character in a dictionary, you need to use its very first stroke, '一', as the indexing component and, by taking away that indexing component, 4 should be the stroke count for the remainder.

2. Occasionally, if two strokes in a character are connected by one stroke hanging over another stroke without affecting the structure and stroke count of the character in question, then this character can be disassembled.
Example: 孝
It can be disassembled into '耂' and '子', and '子' should be used as the indexing component.

3. If a character can be disassembled into parts naturally, but none of the parts are characters themselves or can be used to construct other characters, do not disassemble it.
Example: 非
Do not disassemble it into left and right parts. To locate it in a dictionary, use its first stroke ' 丨 ' as the indexing component, and then 7 should be the stroke count of the remainder.

4. If a character-component has been somehow stretched when it is used to construct another character, after the disassembly, the

(component) character should be restored to its original form.
Example 1: 裹
It should be disassembled into '衣' and '果'.
Example 2: 乘
It should be disassembled into '禾' and '北'.

Radical Identification

1. The radical is generally located at the top, or at the bottom, or on the left, or on the right, or on the outside of a character. For example, the radical '艹' is at the top of the character 花; '女' at the bottom of 妻; '舟' on the left of 船; '彐' on the right of 归; '囗' on the outside of 国.

2. The radical may be located around about the middle of a character if it cannot be found from the 5 positions mentioned above. For example, '田' is the radical of the character 电; '大' the radical of 奉.

3. Examine the four corners of a character if the radical of the character in question cannot be found from all the 6 positions mentioned above. For example, '厶' is the radical of the character 能; '衣' the radical of 裁; '羽' the radical of 翅; '疋' the radical of 疑.

4. For those characters whose radicals are difficult to identify, such as 串, 孝, and 非 as shown in the previous section, it is always a good idea to try to locate them in a dictionary by means of their first strokes. The tables in the next section include 5 one-stroke radicals: '一', '丨', '丿', '丶', and '乙'. For example, '一' is the radical of the character 孝; '丨' the radical of 非; '丿' the radical of 及; '丶' the radical of 为; '乙' the radical of 飞.

The Last Resort

In most Chinese dictionaries, there is actually a 'last resort' indexing table, stroke index for difficult-to-locate characters, that maps the stroke counts to the characters for a few hundred characters which are deemed to be difficult to determine their radicals. The key to using this special indexing table is to correctly work out the stroke counts of those characters that you find very hard to identify their radicals. For example, on the stroke index table in ***The Newly Compiled Elementary Student Dictionary***, you can find the character 串 under stroke count 7 and 非 under stroke count 8, respectively.

More Examples

Character	Indexing Component (IC)	Stroke Count of IC	Remainder (RM)	Stroke Count of RM
闲 (*xián*)	门	3	木	4
爱 (*ài*)	爫	4	夋	6
受 (*shòu*)	爫	4	叐	4
	又	2	爫	6
夏 (*xià*)	夂	3	百	7
吴 (*wú*)	口	3	天	4
天 (*tiān*)	一	1	大	3
	大	3	一	1
连 (*lián*)	辶	2	车	4
孝 (*xiào*)	子	2	耂	4
裹 (*guǒ*)	衣	6	果	8
乘 (*chéng*)	禾	5	北	5

6.5 Lists of 190 Radicals with Character Examples

One stroke

Radical	Name	Examples
一	one	一 丁 万
丨	line	上 也 中
丿	slash	入 九 久
丶	dot	义 求 农
乙 (乛 亅 乚)	second	乙 了 电 事

Two strokes

Radical	Name	Examples
二	two	二 干 于
十	ten	十 千 午
厂	cliff	厂 厅 历

Radical	Name	Examples
匚	right open box	区 巨 医
刂	standing knife	刚 划 创
卜	divination	卜 上 处
冂	down box	内 丹 再
亻	standing man	亿 化 们
八 (丷)	eight	八 六 前
人 (入)	man	人 入 今
勹	wrap	勺 匀 包
几	table	几 风 亮
儿	legs	儿 元 兄
亠	lid	亡 市 交
冫	ice	习 冬 冰
冖	cover	冗 写 军
讠	short form of 言 (speech)	话 说 请
卩	seal	印 危 却
left 阝	short form of 阜 (mound)	阳 阴 院
right 阝	short form of 邑 (city)	那 邮 都
凵	open box	击 出 画
刀 (⺈)	knife	刀 刃 色
力	power	力 加 男
厶	private	么 去 能
又	again	又 叉 难
廴	long stride	廷 延 建

Three strokes

Radical	Name	Examples
工	work	工 左 巧
土	earth	土 去 坏
士	scholar	士 声 喜
扌	short form of 手 (hand)	打 扔 扫
艹	grass	艺 节 花
寸	inch	寸 对 寺
廾	two hands	异 弄 弃
大	big	夫 天 奖
尢	lame	尤 龙 就
弋	shoot	式 贰
小	small	小 少 光
口	mouth	口 叶 古
囗	enclosure	囚 因 国
巾	turban	巾 市 帽

山	mountain	山 岛 岸
彳	step	行 很 得
彡	bristle	形 须 彩
犭	short form of 犬 (dog)	狗 猫 猛
夕	evening	夕 多 夜
夂 (夊)	go	处 冬 夏
饣	short form of 食 (eat)	饭 饮 饿
广	dotted cliff	广 床 库
忄	standing heart	忆 忙 怕
门	gate	门 问 闻
氵	short form of 水 (water)	河 泪 酒
宀	roof	它 牢 家
辶	walk	边 远 进
彐	snout	归 当 录
尸	corpse	尸 尽 层
己 (已 巳)	oneself	己 已 巳 巴
弓	bow	弓 引 弯
子	child	子 孕 孙
女	woman	女 妈 妻
纟	standing silk	红 练 绿
马	horse	马 驶 骂
幺	tiny	乡 幻 幽
川 (巛)	river	川 州 巡

Four strokes

Radical	Name	Examples
王	king	王 玉 全
韦	tanned leather	韦 韧 韬
木	tree	木 本 林
犬	dog	犬 状 哭
歹	death	歹 列 死
车	cart	车 轨 轻
戈	halberd	戈 成 戏
比	compare	比 毕 皆
瓦	tile	瓦 瓮 瓶
止	stop	止 正 此
日	sun	日 早 时
曰	say	曰 曲 冒
水	water	水 永 泉
贝	shell	贝 负 财

见	see	见 观 规
牛	cow	牛 告 物
手	hand	手 承 拿
毛	fur	毛 毫 毯
气	steam	气 氢 氧
攵 (攴)	rap	收 敌 敲
片	slice	片 版 牌
斤	axe	斤 欣 断
爪 (爫)	claw	爪 爬 爱
父	father	父 爷 爸
月	moon	月 有 胖
欠	owe	欠 欲 歌
风	wind	风 飒 飘
殳	weapon	殳 段 毁
文	script	文 斋 斑
方	square	方 放 旁
火	fire	火 灭 灯
斗	dipper	斗 料 斜
灬	short form of 火 (fire)	杰 热 照
户	door	户 房 雇
礻	short form of 示 (spirit)	视 祸 福
心	heart	心 忘 想
聿 (聿)	brush	聿 肃 隶
毋 (母)	do not	毋 母 毒

Five strokes

Radical	Name	Examples
示	spirit	示 票 禁
石	stone	石 矿 硬
龙	dragon	龙 垄 袭
业	trade	业 凿
目	eye	目 看 眼
田	field	田 龟 画
罒	short form of 网 (net)	罗 罚 罢
皿	dish	皿 盆 盐
钅	metal	钉 钟 银
矢	arrow	矢 知 疑
禾	grain	禾 季 秒
白	white	白 百 的
瓜	melon	瓜 瓢 瓣

用	use	用 甩 甫
鸟	bird	鸟 鸡 鸣
疒	sickness	疗 病 痛
立	stand	立 产 站
穴	cave	穴 空 窗
衤	short form of 衣 (clothes)	初 被 裙
疋	bolt of cloth	疋 蛋 疑
皮	skin	皮 皱 颇
矛	spear	矛 柔
癶	dotted tent	癸 登
生	life	生 牲 胜

Six strokes

Radical	**Name**	**Examples**
耒	plough	耕 耘 耗
老	old	老 考
耳	ear	耳 取 聋
臣	minister	臣 卧
西	west	西 要 票
页	leaf	页 顶 顺
虍	tiger	虎 虐 虚
虫	insect	虫 虾 蛇
缶	jar	缶 缸 缺
舌	tongue	舌 乱 舒
竹	bamboo	竹 笔 笑
臼	mortar	臼 舀 舅
自	self	自 臭 鼻
血	blood	血 衄
舟	boat	舟 盘 船
衣	clothes	衣 表 衰
羊	sheep	羊 差 养
米	rice	米 类 糖
艮	stopping	艮 良 即
羽	feather	羽 翅 翼
而	and	而 耍 耐
肉	meat	肉 腐
至	arrive	至 致 到
色	colour	色 艳
糸	silk	系 素 紧

Seven strokes

Radical	Name	Examples
麦	wheat	麦 麸
走	run	走 起 趣
赤	red	赤 郝 赫
豆	bean	豆 豇 登
酉	wine	酉 配 醉
辰	morning	辰 辱 唇
豕	pig	豕 象 豪
里	village	里 重 量
足	foot	足 跑 路
身	body	身 射 躺
采	distinguish	采 悉 释
谷	valley	谷 欲 豁
豸	badger	豺 豹 貌
角	horn	角 触 解
言	speech	言 誉 警
辛	bitter	辛 辜 辫

Eight strokes

Radical	Name	Examples
青	blue	青 靖 静
其	that	其 基 期
雨	rain	雨 雪 雷
齿	tooth	齿 龄 龇
隹	short tailed bird	隹 难 售
金	metal	金 鉴
鱼	fish	鱼 鲜 鲸

Nine strokes

Radical	Name	Examples
革	leather	革 鞋 鞭
骨	bone	骨 骷 髅
鬼	ghost	鬼 魂 魅
食	eat	食 餐
音	sound	音 韵 韶
面	face	面 缅 腼

Ten strokes

Radical	Name	Examples
髟	hair	髦 髯 鬃

Eleven strokes

Radical	Name	Examples
麻	hemp	麻 磨 糜
鹿	deer	鹿 麒 麓

Twelve strokes

Radical	Name	Examples
黑	black	黑 墨 默

Thirteen strokes

Radical	Name	Examples
鼠	rat	鼠 鼬

Fourteen strokes

Radical	Name	Examples
鼻	nose	鼻 鼾

Computer Processing of Chinese Characters

7

汉字的计算机处理

"Part of the inhumanity of the computer is that, once it is competently programmed and working smoothly, it is completely honest."
            novelist and biochemist Isaac Asimov

This book covers almost all the aspects of Chinese characters, but you would have felt it incomplete if it did not mention how to record and process Chinese characters in computers.

All the writing systems in the world were initially invented to record information and assist communications, and have apparently done their job marvellously over thousands of years. The inventions of paper and printing have enabled the writing systems to do their job in a way that the original ancient inventors of the writing systems could never have imagined, and the civilization of mankind (as we are experiencing today) is unimaginable without paper and printing technology. Computers only came into existence around the middle of the 20th century, but their impacts on the communications, archive/retrieval, sharing and processing of information have been unprecedented. It is not an exaggeration to say that, in generations to come, the rapid development of computer and information technology will advance civilization at such a speed and to such a level that could not previously have been predicted.

Information technology, at its core, relies on the writing systems, and processes information in all the human languages. In this sense, it could be argued that the development of various character sets and encoding systems is part of the evolution of the writing systems themselves.

For today's computers, the Chinese writing system is not a natural and easy fit. This is not surprising as: 1) computers were invented based on using alphanumeric characters; 2) English is the de facto language for developing computer related technologies;

3) words in English (and any other phonetic writing system) are a linear composition of alphabetic letters, but Chinese characters are composed two-dimensionally from strokes within a square. However, computer technology is advancing at an unprecedented rate, and the Chinese writing system may one day prove itself invaluable to the development of computer and information technologies.

Currently, one would not think twice when using a normal keyboard to type a letter or report in English. However, when a letter in Chinese needs to be drafted using a word processor, the first thing that would come into one's mind is probably "How do I use my keyboard to input Chinese characters into the computer?" Actually there are already quite a few Chinese character input methods available. This chapter will introduce some of the existing Chinese character input methods as well as briefly discuss some fundamental concepts related to processing Chinese characters in today's computers.

Figure 7.1: Search 汉字 (*hanzi*) and render the results in simplified Chinese characters.

Figure 7.2: Search 漢字 (*hanzi*) and render the results in complex Chinese characters.

7.1 Data Representation in Computers

In today's world, the word 'data' is used almost everywhere and everyday, but what exactly is data? Its most common definition in English dictionaries is information, or a set of facts.

To represent data on paper, we have to use a combination of different writing symbol systems — numeric digits (for numbers), linguistic characters (for words), scientific and mathematical symbols, special characters, and others. Out of all these symbol systems, the linguistic system is the most complicated one, as we have over 100 different language writing systems in the world. For the Chinese writing system alone, it has contained tens of thousands of different characters.

To store and process data in computers, data has to be converted (by means of a coding process) into a form that can be handled by computers — the binary digital form. In other words, data has to be represented by binary code (with only 0's and 1's). In actual fact, we are very accustomed to this kind of coding (mapping/converting) process. English, for example, has got hundreds of thousands of different words, but when it comes down to their compositions, there are only 26 different alphabetic characters in it. That in itself is a type of coding — using a limited number of characters to represent all the words. As long as we have a commonly accepted standard about how to convert data, representing data in binary format in computers should be a relatively easy task. This is where character sets such as ASCII, EBCDIC and Unicode are used.

Now, let us see how data is coded into binary representation.

We all know that the length of English words can be very varied: the shortest ones have just one character (such as a, I), but the majority of English words have two or more characters. Therefore, in a similar way, many bits (**bit** = **b**inary dig**it**) must be combined together to represent data. This sounds very natural. The next question is how many bits are needed. For English words, there is no rule saying how long or short a (new) word must be. However, for effectively and conveniently storing, representing and processing data inside a computer, we need a fixed unit (a certain number of bits) to work with, and somehow, we have to divide the memory space into measurable equivalent units. This unit is called a **byte**, and it has 8 bits.

It is not difficult to see the beauty, logic and convenience in using a byte as a unit measurement for data representation inside a computer:

- It is a power of 2.
- With 8 bits in a byte, it can accommodate 256 (2^8) different representations.
- It opens up the possibilities of multi-byte representations, such as 16-bit machines (2 bytes), 32-bit machines (4 bytes) and 64-bit machines (8 bytes).

With its capability for 256 different representations, one byte is able to represent all the alphanumeric characters and some special characters, such as '+', '-', '%' and '?', see the coding scheme ASCII in Appendix III for example. Evidently, coding schemes such as ASCII and EBCDIC were adequate for handling English words and for computing in the early days of the computer. During my university days in the late 1970s and the early 1980s in China, as I can still vividly remember, the computer was like a giant machine compared to today's desktop computers, but unbelievably less powerful and extremely difficult to use for inputting data and programming code into it. The computer also needed a dedicated and clean room, with a controlled temperature. We learnt how to punch holes onto tapes for preparing data and programs. The computer languages we learnt then were ALGOL and FORTRAN. There were no such applications as word processors. The computers were only used for scientific numerical computations, and alphanumeric characters were all they needed to understand.

To recap, to represent data in computer memory, the memory space needs to be divided into equal units of 1 byte (8 bits), and then every byte can be used to represent one symbol. For example, to store the word 'Chinese', 7 bytes of memory space are needed. With ASCII encoding scheme, the 7 character codes (see the next section for the definition of character code) and their bit representations are shown in the table below

Character	C	h	i	n
Code (Hex)	43	68	69	6E
Bit Representation	1000011	1101000	1101001	1101110
Character	e	s	e	
Code (Hex)	65	73	65	
Bit Representation	1100101	1110011	1100101	

There now comes the question as to how the two characters '中文' — the translation of 'Chinese' — can be stored in computers. It is not difficult to see that 1 byte (8 bits, with 256 different possible representations) is far from enough to handle all the Chinese characters. Unicode (discussed later) uses a combination of 2-byte and 4-byte memory blocks to represent characters in *hanzi*. The 2 character codes and their bit representations for '中文' are given below

Character	中	文
Code (Hex)	4E2D	6587
Bit Representation	100111000101101	110010110000111

7.2 Character Sets and Encoding

ASCII and EBCDIC are two of the most well-known and earliest character sets.

A character set actually embodies two aspects: a collection of characters which include all the linguistic characters from one specific script or a group of scripts, and an encoding scheme in which each character in the set has been uniquely assigned a numerical value — 'character code'. So whenever we talk about a character set, it can be the character set as a collection of characters, or a collection of character codes, or both.

It is well known that both ASCII (which is listed in Appendix III) and EBCDIC only provide support for English, and each of them defines its own (one to one) mapping scheme to map an individual character within the set to a unique numerical value that can be accommodated by a single byte. This is the key to representing data and storing data inside a computer or on any other digital data storage media. The process of mapping characters to numerical numbers is called encoding, or, sometimes, converting.

With more than one encoding scheme in use, a character can be converted into different numerical values, just like a character can be rendered with many different styles. However, human beings are used to the different artistic presentations of characters, as it is an art; the history of Chinese calligraphy goes back some two thousand years. For the information exchange and processing in computers, many different encoding schemes give rise to a lot of problems. That was one of the main reasons why Unicode encoding was introduced.

It is important to bear in mind that, as the encoding scheme used by a character set always specifies the maximum number of bits for encoding all the characters in the set, it is sometimes very convenient to refer to a character set by its maximum number of allowable bits. For instance, ASCII is a 7-bit character set; EBCDIC is an 8-bit character set; you may have also heard of double-byte character sets etc.

7.3 Chinese Character Set and Unicode

It is obvious that Chinese character encoding is needed for handling Chinese characters, used in the Chinese, Japanese, and Korean languages (collectively called CJK), in computers. The main encoding schemes for Chinese characters include:
- GB18030, used in mainland China, is a one, two or four-byte encoding.
- Big5, used in Taiwan and Hong Kong, is a one or two-byte encoding.
- Unicode is also a one, two or four-byte encoding.

7.3.1 Chinese character set

Guobiao, abbreviated as GB and used in the People's Republic of China (PRC), is short for:
- *Guojia Biaozhun*, meaning the 'National Standards', or
- *Guojia Biaozhun Ma*, meaning the 'National Standard Encoding' (of Chinese characters).

Like ANSI in the US, GB standards fall in many areas. Mandatory standards are prefixed by 'GB'. Recommended standards are prefixed by 'GB/T' where the letter 'T' is taken from Chinese *pinyin tuijian* (recommended). Then a standard number follows 'GB' or 'GB/T'. GB is issued by the Standardization Administration of China (SAC) — the Chinese National Committee of the ISO and IEC.

In the context of Chinese character encoding, 'GB' alone is often used to indicate GB2312-80 (GB2312 for short, issued in 1980 and put into force in 1981), or GB18030-2000 (GB18030 for short, issued in 2000 and put into force in 2001), both of which are used in mainland China and Singapore. GB2312 was created to encode simplified Chinese characters, and it has included 6763 *hanzi*.[1] GB18030 is a new character set standard from the PRC that specifies an extended character set and a mapping table to Unicode. In 2000, the Chinese government issued regulations mandating that all the operating systems on non-handheld computers sold in the PRC after January 1, 2001 (later postponed to September 1, 2001) would have to comply with the new multi-byte GB18030 standard. GB18030 contains 27533 Chinese characters (both simplified and complex).[2]

Unlike mainland China, Taiwan and Hong Kong, where complex Chinese characters (traditional Chinese characters) are used, have adopted Big5 as the encoding standard. Big5 includes 13053 *hanzi*.

7.3.2 Unicode

What is Unicode? The Unicode Consortium provides the clear answer: "Fundamentally, computers just deal with numbers. They store letters and other characters by assigning a number for each one. Before Unicode was invented, there were hundreds of different encoding systems for assigning these numbers.... *Unicode provides a unique number for every character, no matter what the platform, no matter what the program, no matter what the language....* The emergence of the Unicode Standard, and the availability of tools supporting it, are among the most significant recent global software technology trends." [3]

Another important aim of Unicode is to provide lossless conversion amongst different existing encodings. The reason for this is very simple: there are many different encoding systems in use, and as ever, there are many different standards.

Despite its technical limitations and criticisms, Unicode has emerged as the de facto encoding scheme to internationalize software and multilingual environments. For example, to represent multilingual text internally, Microsoft Windows NT and its descendants such as Windows 2000 and Windows XP have adopted Unicode UTF-16; UNIX, Linux, BSD and Mac OS X have adopted Unicode UTF-8.

Unicode merges all the major Chinese character set standards prior to GB18030-2000 into one larger repertoire and enumerates a total of 20,902 unique characters — including Chinese *hanzi*, Japanese *Kanji*, Korean *Hanja*, and Vietnamese *Chu Nom* (CJKV). Chinese characters that differ only in glyphs [†] are often combined to occupy a single point.

7.4 Inputting Chinese Characters into Computers

A variety of keyboard input methods have been designed to allow the input of Chinese characters using standard keyboards. Other means of inputting Chinese characters are not as widely used but include stylus and tablet, OCR and voice recognition. As with any language, all these non-keyboard based methods suffer different kinds of problems and have not been accepted for daily use on desktop computers by the general public.

Keyboard input methods can be classified into three main types:
- encoding method, for instance by means of Unicode
- phonetic method , the *Pinyin* method is very popular albeit slow
- structural method, see the *Wubi* method below

It should be emphasized that different people are comfortable with different input methods and each method has its strengths and

[†] A glyph is an image of a character in a particular font, style and size. For instance, the character 'h' can be rendered in many different glyphs: '**h**' — bold, '*h*' — italic, '***h***' — bold and italic etc.

weaknesses. For example, for someone who is already familiar with *pinyin*, the *Pinyin* method can be learnt almost instantly; however, the maximum typing rate is limited. On the other hand, the *Wubi* method takes a lot of effort to learn and is easy to forget if not used for a while; but with this method, expert typists can type much faster than using the phonetic methods. Because of these various factors, there is not yet a 'standard' keyboard input method. A brief introduction to some of the keyboard input methods is given below.

Pinyin

Pinyin, short for *Pinyin* input method, is the easiest and most commonly used Chinese character input method at present. As mentioned earlier, to use this input method efficiently, one must understand the *pinyin* system and needs to be able to speak Mandarin correctly. This method has some variations, such as the Full *Pinyin* and Double *Pinyin* methods.

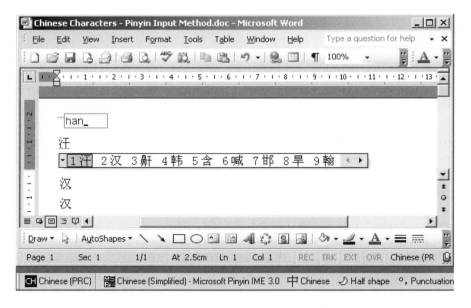

Figure 7.3: The input of the character 汉 by *Pinyin* method.

As homophony is a key feature of Chinese characters, or in other words a Chinese sound may correspond to a group of different Chinese characters, more often than not the method will require the user to select a character from a pop-up list of different characters with the same sound.

Figure 7.3 demonstrates how to input the character 汉 (*han*) into a computer: 1) enable the *Pinyin* input method; 2) type in 'han' and then press the 'space bar' to indicate the end of the input: a character with the sound of '*han*' will appear, which may or may not be the character expected — in this example the appeared character is 汗; 3) as the appeared character is not what we want, a pop-up list of all the homophonic characters (with the sound '*han*') can be brought up by pressing the left-arrow key; 4) as the character we wanted is the second on the pop-up list, we can either type 2 or select the character directly with the mouse; 5) the dotted line beneath the character indicates the character just entered/selected has not been accepted yet, it can then be accepted by pressing 'space bar' again.

Wubi

Wubi, short for *Wubizixing* input method, was invented by *Wang Yongmin* in 1983 [4] and is based on the structure of Chinese characters. Unlike any phonetic input method, the *Wubi* method is not linked to any particular Chinese dialect, and it is also very effective for inputting unfamiliar characters. With this method, every character that one would like to use can be entered with 5 keystrokes at most. In practice, most characters can actually be inputted with less than 5 keystrokes.

It should be noted that the name *Wubi*, which literally means 'five strokes', has nothing to do with number of strokes. It is just based on the way the method works: [†]

1) Disassemble Chinese characters into some 200 'character roots' (they are different from character components in concept, but the majority of which are actually the indexing components, see Chapter 6 — **Looking up Characters in a Dictionary**), and logically group these 200 roots into 5 categories.

2) As demonstrated in Figure 7.4, reserve the '*Z*' key as a wild key, and then divide the other 25 keys into 5 zones

[†] All the discussions on *Wubi* method in this chapter are based on *Wubi* standard *Wubi*86.

accordingly. Each of the 5 zones will be used for mapping one specific category of character roots. In this way, each of the 25 keys is mapped with, on average, 8 roots (actually, the keys *'E'* and *'Q'* have both got the maximum number of roots — 12, and the keys *'S'* and *'K'* have got the minimum number of roots — 3).

3) According to the rules of *hanzi* writing (see Chapter 4 — **Writing *Hanzi***), each Chinese character can now be broken into a sequential combination of some (3 or 4, in most cases) roots from a pool of 200 character roots.

4) Based on the mapping mentioned above and with some special enhancement rules, each character can then be uniquely encoded into a combination of 4 letters.

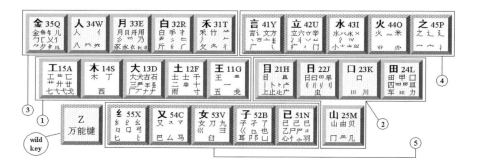

Figure 7.4: *Wubi* keyboard layout.

Figure 7.5: *Wubi* encoding for Chinese character 适.

For example, the Chinese character 适, as shown in Figure 7.5, can be broken down into three letters 'TDP'. The *Wubi* encoding rule for three-letter Chinese characters is to add a 4th letter by means of the concept of 'last stroke'. In this case, the letter representing its 'last stroke' is 'D', therefore the *Wubi* encoding for 适 is 'TDPD'.

Cangjie

Cangjie, short for *Cangjie* input method, was invented in 1976 by *Chu Bong-Foo* (which is pronounced *Zhū Bāngfù* in *pinyin*) in Taiwan.[5] The method is named after *Cang Jie*, who, in legend, is usually attributed with the invention of the ancient Chinese characters (see Chapter 1). Similar to *Wubi*, but unlike *Pinyin*, the *Cangjie* method is based on the structural aspect of the characters — components and strokes.

Four Corner

Four Corner, short for Four Corner input method, is based on a method that encodes Chinese characters using four numerical digits per character (in some situations, an additional digit is used).

In the 1920s, *Wang Yunwu*, the editor-in-chief of the Commercial Press of China back then, invented 'Four Corner Indexing' to index Chinese characters in dictionaries;[6] the method was very popular before the wide spread use of *pinyin*.

Before we finish off this chapter, Table 7-1 uses 10 Chinese characters to demonstrate the various encodings discussed in this chapter.

Hanzi	*Pinyin*	**Meaning in English**	**GB18030 and Unicode**	**Encodings for Computer Input**
高	*gāo*	high; tall	B8DF U+9AD8	*Wubi*: YMKF *Cangjie*: 卜口月口 (YRBR) Four Corner: 0022_7
憨	*hān*	foolish; straightforward	BAA9 U+61A8	*Wubi*: NBTN *Cangjie*: 一大心 (MKP) Four Corner: 1833_4
多	*duō*	much; many	B6E0 U+591A	*Wubi*: QQU *Cangjie*: 弓戈弓戈 (NINI) Four Corner: 2720_7
津	*jīn*	ford; saliva	BDF2 U+6D25	*Wubi*: IVFH *Cangjie*: 水中手 (ELQ) Four Corner: 3510_7

架	jià	rack; shelf	BCDC U+67B6	*Wubi*: LKSU *Cangjie*: 大口木 (KRD) Four Corner: 4690_4
拍	pāi	clap; beat	C5C4 U+62CD	*Wubi*: RRG *Cangjie*: 手竹日 (QHA) Four Corner: 5600_0
黑	hēi	black; dark	BADA U+9ED1	*Wubi*: LFOU *Cangjie*: 田土火 (WGF) Four Corner: 6033_1
胎	tāi	foetus; tyre	CCA5 U+80CE	*Wubi*: ECKG *Cangjie*: 月戈口 (BIR) Four Corner: 7326_0
气	qì	gas; air; steam	C6F8 U+6C14	*Wubi*: RNB *Cangjie*: 人一弓 (OMN) Four Corner: 8001_7
悔	huǐ	repent; regret	BBDA U+6094	*Wubi*: NTXU *Cangjie*: 心人田卜 (POWY) Four Corner: 9805_5

Table 7-1: Examples of encoding Chinese characters.

Translating Names into Chinese

8

外文名字的中文翻译

"Words — so innocent and powerless as they are, as standing in a dictionary, how potent for good and evil they become in the hands of one who knows how to combine them!"
Nathaniel Hawthorne (*The American Notebooks*)

Languages are the exceedingly rich and complex assets of human beings. This very richness makes translation, say from a foreign language to Chinese or vice versa, a challenging and delicate operation. However, this chapter is not going to talk about how to translate, but, via some interesting examples, to present a special and unique area in translation — translating foreign names into Chinese. The emphasis, rather than on the principles of translation, is on how Chinese characters can be applied in translated names with an excellent combination of fidelity and creativity.

Names — be they for people, for countries or places, for business entities, or for brands — are something we love and hate, something we cannot live without, something that at times are too many to manage.

Foreign names present an extra layer of difficulty with not only language but also culture and custom to people in any country. It is therefore very important to have foreign names translated accordingly.

Normally, names can be translated using four different approaches:
1) to transliterate — to translate by imitating the sounds
2) to translate the meanings
3) to translate literally — to translate word-by-word
4) to translate by mixing all three

In the following sections, we'll examine how the above approaches can be used to great effect in translating names of people, countries, places, business entities and brands.

8.1 Names of People

In China, foreign names are translated into Chinese equivalents according to their sounds. There are handbooks of foreign names for languages such as English, French, German, Italian and Spanish etc., see *A Dictionary of English Names* [1] for example.

A list of common British and American names can also be found in major dictionaries such as *A New English-Chinese Dictionary* [2] and *Great English-Chinese Dictionary*.[3]

Name in English	Name in Chinese	*Pinyin* of Family Name
Ludwig Van Beethoven	路德维希·凡·贝多芬	*Bèiduōfēn*
Napoleon Bonaparte	拿破仑·波拿巴	*Nápòlún* (拿破仑)
Charlie Chaplin	查理·卓别林	*Zhuóbiélín*
Winston Churchill	温思顿·丘吉尔	*Qiūjíěr*
Christopher Columbus	克里斯托弗·哥伦布	*Gēlúnbù*
Charles Darwin	查尔斯·达尔文	*Dáěrwén*
Thomas Alva Edison	托马斯·阿尔瓦·爱迪生	*Àidíshēng*
Albert Einstein	艾伯特·爱因斯坦	*Àiyīnsītǎn*
Henry Ford	亨利·福特	*Fútè*
Sigmund Freud	西格蒙德·弗洛伊德	*Fúluòyīdé*
Abraham Lincoln	亚伯拉罕·林肯	*Línkěn*
Martin Luther King	马丁·路德·金	*Jīn*
Isaac Newton	艾萨克·牛顿	*Níudùn*
Pablo Picasso	帕布罗·毕加索	*Bìjiāsuǒ*
Franklin Delano Roosevelt	富兰克林·德拉诺·罗斯福	*Luósīfú*
William Shakespeare	威廉·莎士比亚	*Shāshìbǐyà*
Adam Smith	亚当·史密斯	*Shǐmìsī*
Leonardo da Vinci	列奥纳多·达·芬奇	*Dáfēnqí* (达·芬奇)

Table 8-1: Some of the most influential people outside of China from the last millennium.

Table 8-1 lists some of the most influential people outside of China from the last millennium and their names in Chinese. From the list, a few basic principles in translating foreign names into Chinese equivalents can be observed:

1) The order of names (first name, surname, etc.) in a translated name always follows that in the original one. For example, William Shakespeare is known as 威廉·莎士比亚 in Chinese, in which 威廉 is the Chinese equivalent of William, and 莎士比亚 Shakespeare. What is special about this? Well, in Chinese names, surnames always appear first, but translated (foreign) names need not follow this name ordering convention.

2) Translated names should sound and look very 'foreign'. Most Chinese names have a very unique and subtle meaning. However, a translated name only imitates the sound, and the combination of the Chinese characters adopted in it has been deliberately made meaningless.

3) If possible, the sound in the original language should be imitated.

4) The end result should be succinct.

8.2 Names of Countries or Places

Generally speaking, names of countries or places are translated in the same way as names of people are translated: they are normally translated according to their sounds. Similar to translating people's names, the following rules should normally but not always be followed when it comes to translating names of countries or places:

1) Imitate the sound in the local language if possible.

2) If there exists a translation for the country/place in question and the translation does not entirely follow the first rule, keep using the existing one.

3) The translated name should sound 'foreign' but meaningless.

4) The end result should be succinct.

Table 8-2 shows the Chinese names of 10 countries.

The Chinese names of Australia, Canada and Spain — 澳大利亚, 加拿大 and 西班牙, respectively — were derived from their sounds in the local languages. For Iceland — 冰岛, it was translated directly, where 冰 is the Chinese character for ice, and 岛 is the Chinese character for island. In the case of New Zealand — 新西兰, the two words in the name were handled differently: 'New' was directly translated into 新, 'Zealand' was transliterated by two

Chinese characters 西兰. For Poland — 波兰, it was phonetically imitated from the English pronunciation, rather than from *Polska* in Polish.

Name in English	Name in Local Language	Name in Chinese	Pronunciation of Chinese Name
America	America	美国	*Měiguó*
Australia	Australia	澳大利亚	*Àodàlìyà*
Canada	Canada	加拿大	*Jiānádà*
England	England	英国	*Yīngguó*
France	France (in French)	法国	*Fǎguó*
Germany	Deutschland (in German)	德国	*Déguó*
Iceland	Ísland (in Icelandic)	冰岛	*Bīngdǎo*
New Zealand	New Zealand	新西兰	*Xīnxīlán*
Poland	Polska (in Polish)	波兰	*Bōlán*
Spain	España (in Spanish)	西班牙	*Xībānyá*

Table 8-2: Some countries and their Chinese names.

The Chinese names of America, England, France and Germany — 美国, 英国, 法国 and 德国, respectively — are four of some of the special cases in all the translated country names. Each of them was made up by combining two Chinese characters — the first one partially imitates the sound and the second one is the Chinese character for country (国). Another interesting point about the Chinese names of these four countries is that the original translators had made an effort to use complimentary characters to partially imitate the sounds. Let us examine these four names one by one:
  1) America (美国, *Měiguó*) — 'country of beauty'
      • 美 is pronounced *měi* in Chinese, which sounds similar to the second syllable 'me' in the word America.
      • 美 means beautiful in Chinese.

2) England (英国, *Yīngguó*) — 'country of wisdom'
   - 英 is pronounced *yīng* in Chinese, which sounds identical to the beginning of the word England.
   - 英 means wisdom and heroic in Chinese.
3) France (法国, *Fǎguó*) — 'country of law'
   - 法 is pronounced *fǎ* in Chinese, and the syllable begins with *f*.
   - 法 means law and rules in Chinese.
4) Germany (德国, *Déguó*) — 'country of virtue'
   - Germany is called Deutschland in German. 德 is pronounced *dé* in Chinese.
   - 德 means virtue in Chinese.

Name in English	Name in Local Language	Name in Chinese	Pronunciation of Chinese Name
Amsterdam	Amsterdam (in Dutch)	阿姆斯特丹	*Āmǔsītèdān*
Berlin	Berlin (in German)	柏林	*Bólín*
Lisbon	Lisboa (in Portuguese)	里斯本	*Lǐsīběn*
London	London	伦敦	*Lúndūn*
Moscow	Москва (in Russian)	莫斯科	*Mòsīkè*
New York	New York	纽约	*Niǔyuē*
Paris	Paris (in French)	巴黎	*Bālí*
Rome	Roma (in Italian)	罗马	*Luómǎ*
Sydney	Sydney	悉尼	*Xīní*
Toronto	Toronto	多伦多	*Duōlúnduō*

Table 8-3: Some large international cities and their Chinese names.

Table 8-3 shows the translated names of 10 large international cities. The Chinese names for all the cities but Lisbon and Moscow came from the sounds in their local languages. For Lisbon, the Chinese name 里斯本 sounds closer to the English pronunciation of Lisbon than to the sound of Lisbon in Portuguese (*Lisboa*); in the case of Moscow, the Chinese name 莫斯科 sounds closer to Moscow than to *Москва*.

These examples have vividly demonstrated that, although imitating sounds in the local languages should have been the main rule of translating names of countries or places, the existence of an earlier translation, even though not sounding similar, normally guarantees an adoption.

8.3 Names of Business Entities

Choosing a name for a company is a serious matter. Some people may not have fully appreciated the importance of business names, but research has shown that the business name is one of the most important intangible assets of a company.

When it comes to choosing a name, companies normally take the following factors into consideration:
- branding
- easy to read, write and remember
- succinct and uniquely identifiable
- reflective and associative

If a company decides to expand its business into China, it then has to decide:
- Is it necessary to have a Chinese name for the business?
- How can the name be translated into its Chinese equivalent?

In most cases, it is in a company's best interests to have its name translated. There are a few simple reasons for doing so:
- Various legal reasons may not permit the original name to be registered legitimately in China.
- The company is likely to be referred to in Chinese according to its sound conveniently by the local people, but the Chinese name (or names) adopted may not be what the company wants from a marketing point of view.
- A good translated Chinese name is as important as the company's original name.

How can a company get its name translated into Chinese? Apart from the factors mentioned earlier, the following additional factors also need to be taken into account:

- It should be culturally accepted, and, more importantly, positive;
- It should sound foreign, distinct and cool, and have some degree of resemblance.

Many multi-national companies such as AstraZeneca, B&Q, Carrefour, Cisco Systems, Coca-Cola, Ericsson, Google, Hewlett-Packard, Johnson & Johnson, Microsoft, Motorola, Nestlé and Nokia all have a Chinese name, and they have now become famous household names in China, see Table 8-4.

Company Name in English	Company Name in Chinese	Pronunciation of Chinese Name
AstraZeneca	阿斯利康	*Āsīlìkāng*
B&Q	百安居	*Bǎiānjū*
Carrefour	家乐福	*Jiālèfú*
Cisco Systems	思科	*Sīkē*
Coca-Cola	可口可乐	*Kěkǒukělè*
Ericsson	爱立信	*Àilìxìn*
Google	谷歌	*Gǔgē*
Hewlett-Packard	惠普	*Huìpǔ*
Johnson & Johnson	强生	*Qiángshēng*
Microsoft	微软	*Wēiruǎn*
Motorola	摩托罗拉	*Mótuōluólā*
Nestlé	雀巢	*Quècháo*
Nokia	诺基亚	*Nuòjīyà*

Table 8-4: Some multi-national companies and their names in Chinese.

How did they do the translation? In the rest of this section, we will examine the origins of these 13 companies and their names, their Chinese translations and the unique and subtle meanings in them.

1) AstraZeneca — 阿斯利康 (*Āsīlìkāng*)
AstraZeneca was formed on 6th April 1999 through the merging of Astra AB of Sweden and Zeneca of Britain, and it is now one of the world's leading pharmaceutical companies.[4]

AstraZeneca is known as 阿斯利康 in China.[5]

Analysis: The Chinese name consists of 4 Chinese characters.

- The first two characters — 阿斯 — imitate the beginning sound of AstraZeneca, and they are the same as the first two characters in the well known medicine 阿斯匹林 (the Chinese name for aspirin). The direct impression of the usage is to remind people that the business is related to medicine.
- The last two characters — 利康 — try to imitate the ending sound of AstraZeneca, albeit not as closely as 阿斯 do to the beginning sound, and mean 'good/benefit for the health' in Chinese.

2) B&Q — 百安居 (*Băiānjū*)

B&Q is the UK's leading home improvement and garden centre retailer, and it was co-founded by Richard Block and David Quayle in 1969.[6] The name B&Q is from the initials of Block and Quayle.

B&Q is known as 百安居 in China, and B&Q Beijing is the largest B&Q store in the world.[7]

Analysis: The Chinese name consists of 3 Chinese characters.

- The first character — 百 — is the Chinese character for hundred, and it is pronounced *băi*, which begins with the sound of /b/. Chinese people also use this word to imply many.
- The second character — 安 — is the Chinese word for safe, peace, comfort, setting and installation, and it is pronounced *ān*, which is similar to the sound of '&'.
- The last character — 居 — is the Chinese character for residence and home, and it is pronounced *jū*, of which the beginning sound /j/ is similar to the sound of /q/.

3) Carrefour — 家乐福 (*Jiālèfú*)

Carrefour is one of the world's leading distribution groups.[8] Created by Marcel Fournier and Denis Defforey, the first Carrefour store opened on 3rd June 1957 in suburban Annecy of France near a crossroads (carrefour in French).

Carrefour is known as 家乐福 in China.[9]

Analysis: The Chinese name consists of 3 Chinese characters which imitate the sound of the original name quite well.
- The first character — 家 — is the Chinese word for family, household, home.
- The second character — 乐 — is the Chinese word for happy, joyful and cheerful.
- The third character — 福 — is the Chinese word for good fortune, happiness and blessing.

4) Cisco Systems — 思科 (*Sīkē*)
Cisco Systems is the worldwide leader in networking for the Internet, and it was founded in 1984 by a small group of computer scientists from Stanford University [10] in the USA. The word 'Cisco' does not stem from an acronym but is an abbreviation of San Francisco.

Cisco Systems is known as 思科 in China.[11]

Analysis: The Chinese name consists of 2 Chinese characters which imitate the sound of the original name very well.
- The first character — 思 — is the Chinese word for thinking, thought and idea.
- The second character — 科 — is the Chinese word for science.

5) Coca-Cola — 可口可乐 (*Kěkǒukělè*)
Founded in 1886, Coca-Cola is the world's leading manufacturer, marketer, and distributor of non-alcoholic beverage concentrates and syrups. Coca-Cola was invented in May 1886 by Dr. John S. Pemberton in Atlanta, Georgia of the USA. The name 'Coca-Cola' was suggested by Dr. Pemberton's bookkeeper, Frank Robinson. He penned the name Coca-Cola in the flowing script that is famous today.[12]

Coca-Cola is known as 可口可乐 in China.[13]

Analysis: The Chinese name consists of 4 Chinese characters which imitate the sound of the original name almost perfectly.
- The first two characters — 可口 — mean delicious, tasty and good to eat or drink.

- The last two characters — 可乐 — mean to make you laugh, happy and joyful.

6) Ericsson — 爱立信 (Àilìxìn)

Ericsson is the largest supplier of mobile systems in the world and supports all major standards for wireless communication. The name Ericsson came from its founder Lars Magnus Ericsson.[14]

Ericsson is known as 爱立信 in China.[15]

Analysis: The Chinese name consists of 3 Chinese characters which imitate the sound of the original name closely.

- The first character — 爱 — is the Chinese word for love and affection.
- The second character — 立 — is the Chinese word for establish, exist and set up.
- The last character — 信 — is the Chinese character for trust, believe and reputation. It is also the Chinese character for letter, message and information.

7) Google — 谷歌 (Gǔgē)

Founded in September 1998, Google is now widely recognized as the world's largest search engine — an easy-to-use free service that usually returns relevant results in a fraction of a second. The name Google is a play on the word googol, which refers to the number represented by the numeral 1 followed by 100 zeros.[16]

Google is known as 谷歌 in China.[17]

Analysis: The Chinese name consists of 2 Chinese characters, which imitate the sound of the original name very well.

- The first character — 谷 — is the Chinese word for valley, and also for grain.
- The second character — 歌 — is the Chinese word for song.

8) Hewlett-Packard — 惠普 (Huìpǔ)

Hewlett-Packard is the largest consumer IT company, the world's largest SMB IT company and a leading enterprise IT company. The name Hewlett-Packard came from its two co-founders, Bill Hewlett and Dave Packard, who tossed a coin to decide whether the company they founded would be called Hewlett-Packard or Packard-Hewlett.[18]

Hewlett-Packard is known as 惠普 in China.[19]

Analysis: The Chinese name consists of 2 Chinese characters.
- The first character — 惠 — is the Chinese word for favour, kindness, preference and benefit. It is pronounced *Huì*, which imitates the beginning sound of <u>Hew</u>lett.
- The second character — 普 — is the Chinese word for general, universal, broad and extensive. It is pronounced *Pǔ*, which begins with the sound of /p/.

9) Johnson & Johnson — 强生 (*Qiángshēng*)
Johnson & Johnson is the world's most comprehensive and broadly based manufacturer of health care products, as well as a provider of related services, for the consumer, pharmaceutical, and medical devices and diagnostics markets. It was formed, in 1886, by James Wood Johnson and Edward Mead Johnson in a rented space in New Brunswick, New Jersey of the USA.[20]

Johnson & Johnson is known as 强生 in China.[21]

Analysis: The Chinese name consists of only 2 Chinese characters which imitate the sound of Johnson quite well.
- The first character — 强 — is the Chinese word for strengthening, strong, powerful and energetic.
- The second character — 生 — is the Chinese word for growing, life and lifetime.

10) Microsoft — 微软 (*Wēiruǎn*)
Microsoft is the world's largest software company.[22] Microsoft was founded in Albuquerque, New Mexico of the USA in 1975 under the company name Micro-soft (short for microcomputer software).

Microsoft is known as 微软 in China.[23]

Analysis: The Chinese name consists of 2 Chinese characters. The translated name does not imitate the sound of the original name, but it is the precise translation of the meaning.

- The first character — 微 — is the Chinese word for micro and very small.
- The second character — 软 — is the Chinese word for soft. It should be noted that, the word 'software' is equivalent to Chinese word 软件

11) Motorola — 摩托罗拉 (*Mótuōluólā*)

Motorola, Inc. is a global leader in wireless, broadband and automotive communications technologies and embedded electronic products.[24] Founder Paul Galvin came up with the name *Motorola* — a word suggesting sound in motion — when his company started manufacturing car radios

Motorola is known as 摩托罗拉 in China.[25]

Analysis: The Chinese name consists of 4 Chinese characters which imitate the sound of the original name very well.
- The first two characters — 摩托 — are the Chinese equivalent for motor.
- The last two characters — 罗拉 — only imitate the sound of 'rola'. The phrase does not mean anything specific in Chinese, but sounds very foreign.

12) Nestlé — 雀巢 (*Quècháo*)

Nestlé, whose headquarters is in Vevey, Switzerland, was founded in 1866 by Henri Nestlé and today is the world's biggest food and beverage company.[26] Henri Nestlé was born Heinrich Nestle in 1814, and had his family origin in Swabia. In the Swabian dialect 'Nestle' is a small bird's nest. The company logo of Nestlé consists of small birds, a nest and 'Nestlé'.

Nestlé is known as 雀巢 in China.[27]

Analysis: The Chinese name consists of 2 Chinese characters. The translated name does not imitate the sound of Nestlé, but it is a very nice translation of the meaning conveyed in the original name and the logo.
- The first character — 雀 — is the Chinese word for sparrow.
- The second character — 巢 — is the Chinese word for nest.

13) Nokia — 诺基亚 (*Nuòjīyà*)
Nokia is a world leader in mobile communications, driving the growth and sustainability of the broader mobility industry.[28] Nokia was founded in 1865 as a wood-pulp mill by Fredrik Idestam. The company then expanded into producing rubber products in Nokia, an industrialized town of about 27000 inhabitants in Finland, and began to use *Nokia* as a brand.

Nokia is known as 诺基亚 in China.[29]

Analysis: The Chinese name consists of 3 Chinese characters which imitate the sound of the original name well.
- The combination of the three characters is the actual translation of Nokia as a town in Finland.
- 诺 means promise in Chinese; 基 means base, foundation, basic and key in Chinese; 亚 implies Asia in Chinese.

8.4 Brand Names

Name in English	Name in Chinese	Pronunciation of Chinese Name
Mercedes-Benz	奔驰	*Bēnchí*
Canon	佳能	*Jiānéng*
IKEA	宜家	*Yíjiā*
Titoni	梅花表	*Méihuābiǎo*
TOEFL	托福	*Tuófú*

Table 8-5: Some brand names and their Chinese translations.

1) Mercedes-Benz — 奔驰 (*Bēnchí*)
Mercedes-Benz is an internationally known car brand from DaimlerChrysler.[30] The company gives Mercedes-Benz a Chinese name — 奔驰.[31]
- The name imitates the sound of 'Benz' very closely.
- 奔 is the Chinese word for run fast, rush about and pour down; 驰 is the Chinese word for speed and gallop.
- The company chooses the Chinese characters 奔驰 to imply 'running arrow' and echo its legendary Silver Arrow.

2) Canon — 佳能 (*Jiānéng*)
Canon is a world-renowned brand for imaging and optical products

from Canon Inc.[32] The company gives Canon a Chinese name —
佳能.[33]

- The name imitates the sound of 'Canon' well.
- 佳 is the Chinese word for fine, beautiful, excellent; 能 is the Chinese word for ability, can, able.
- The company chooses the Chinese characters 佳能 to reflect its founding characteristic — precision.

3) IKEA — 宜家 (*Yíjiā*)

IKEA is a brand from Inter IKEA Systems B.V.[34] The company gives IKEA a Chinese name — 宜家.[35]

- IKEA and its Chinese name — 宜家 — contain the same number of syllables, 2 in this case.
- 宜 is the Chinese word for suitable and good for; 家 is the Chinese word for home.

4) Titoni — 梅花表 (*Méihuābiǎo*)

Titoni is a brand name from the Swiss watch manufacturer Titoni Ltd. The company gives its brand a Chinese name 梅花表.[36]

- The first two characters 梅花 are the Chinese word for plum flower, which represents exactly the logo of the company.
- The last character 表 is the Chinese word for watch.

5) TOEFL — 托福 (*Tuófú*)

TOEFL stands for <u>T</u>est <u>o</u>f <u>E</u>nglish as a <u>F</u>oreign <u>L</u>anguage, and is an internationally famous brand from the non-profit ETS.[37] TOEFL is translated into 托福 in Chinese:

- The Chinese name imitates the sound of TOEFL.
- 托 is the Chinese word for rely upon and owe to; 福 is the Chinese word for good fortune and blessing.

Hanzi Study (1): Chinese Words, Idioms and Proverbs
汉字学习（一）：汉语词汇，成语及谚语

9

"The wisdom of the wise and the experience of the ages is preserved into perpetuity by a nation's proverbs, fables, folk sayings and quotations."
American publisher and author William Feather

In the previous chapter, it has been demonstrated that when it comes to translating foreign names into Chinese, more often than not, the translation is either rule based (to imitate sounds, for instance) or just intuitively created (e.g. to translate business or brand names).

In this chapter and the next, some *hanzi* will be examined and, if necessary, analysed by putting them into context such as multi-character words, idioms, proverbs and riddles. These interesting and inspiring explorations will not only enable readers to appreciate Chinese characters at a practical yet higher level, but also demonstrate the rich Chinese culture involved in Chinese characters and the language.

This chapter concentrates on Chinese words, idioms and proverbs. The next chapter introduces and examines some Chinese character riddles. By the end of reading through these two chapters, you may not only have found both chapters very intriguing but also have realized that the Chinese language is not as foreign as you thought.

9.1 Single-Character Words

As has been discussed in previous chapters, Chinese characters are logographic characters; in most cases, each character is a 'word' rather than a 'letter', and each character is a meaningful entity. Single-character Chinese words are also referred to as monosyllabic words.

9.1.1 The twelve animals of the Chinese Zodiac

Hanzi	鼠	牛	虎	兔
Pinyin	shǔ	niú	hǔ	tù
English	rat	ox	tiger	rabbit
Year Index	1	2	3	4
Hanzi	龙	蛇	马	羊
Pinyin	lóng	shé	mǎ	yáng
English	dragon	snake	horse	sheep
Year Index	5	6	7	8
Hanzi	猴	鸡	狗	猪
Pinyin	hóu	jī	gǒu	zhū
English	monkey	rooster	dog	pig
Year Index	9	10	11	12

The 'year index' in the above table is given by the following formulae:

remainder[(year of birth - 1900) / 12] + 1
(from 1900 onwards)

or

13 - remainder[(1900 - year of birth) / 12]
(1899 and earlier)

For example, if someone was born in May 1988, then by using the first formula, the corresponding 'year index' can be readily obtained

remainder[(1988 - 1900) / 12] + 1
= 4 + 1 = 5

From the table, it can then be seen that this person was born in the year of the 'dragon' in the Chinese lunar calendar, or the person was born under the animal sign of 'dragon'.

It should be noted that, since the first day of the Chinese lunar calendar falls between January 21 and February 20 of the Gregorian calendar, special reference to Chinese New Year has to be made when using the above formulae for someone who was born in January or February (see ***Gregorian-Lunar Calendar Conversion Table*** [1] for the beginning dates of Chinese New Year from 1901 to 2100).

9.1.2 Chinese numerals

Hanzi	一	二	三	四	五
Pinyin	*yī*	*èr*	*sān*	*sì*	*wǔ*
English	one	two	three	four	five
Hanzi	六	七	八	九	十
Pinyin	*liù*	*qī*	*bā*	*jiǔ*	*shí*
English	six	seven	eight	nine	ten
Hanzi	百	千	万	亿	
Pinyin	*bǎi*	*qiān*	*wàn*	*yì*	
English	hundred	thousand	ten thousand	hundred million	

By using the above basic Chinese numerals, the following decimal numbers can be readily represented:

15	=	十五
267	=	二百六十七
3874	=	三千八百七十四
8 million	=	八百万
9 billion	=	九十亿

9.1.3 The four seasons

Hanzi	春	夏	秋	冬
Pinyin	*chūn*	*xià*	*qiū*	*dōng*
English	spring	summer	autumn/fall	winter

9.1.4 The four common tastes

Hanzi	甜	酸	苦	辣
Pinyin	tián	suān	kǔ	là
English	sweet	sour	bitter	spicy

9.1.5 Relative positions or directions

Hanzi	上	下	左	右
Pinyin	shàng	xià	zuǒ	yòu
English	up	down	left	right
Hanzi	前	后	中	
Pinyin	qián	hòu	zhōng	
English	front	back	centre	

9.1.6 Compass points

Hanzi	东	西	南	北
Pinyin	dōng	xī	nán	běi
English	east	west	south	north

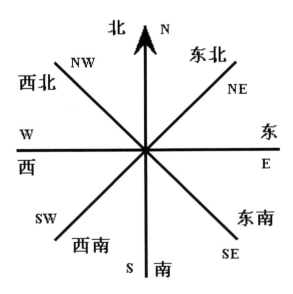

Examine the illustration of compass points, can you noticed
the subtle difference of saying directions between Chinese and
English? In English, people say northeast (NE), northwest (NW),

southeast (SE), and southwest (SW). On the contrary, the Chinese say 东北, 西北, 东南, and 西南, which literally mean east-north, west-north, east-south, and west-south, respectively.

9.2 Multi-Character Words

Chinese words with two characters are called dissyllabic words, and those with more than two characters are called polysyllabic words. Some examples of multi-character words are:

Word	天使	幸福	风水
Pinyin	*tiānshǐ*	*xìngfú*	*fēngshuǐ*
English	angel	happiness	*fengshui*
Word	图书馆	不好意思	
Pinyin	*túshūguǎn*	*bù hǎoyìsi*	
English	library	embarrassment	

Multi-character Chinese words play a vital role in modern Chinese: most of the time, when put into context, Chinese characters will appear in multi-character words rather than individually. Within multi-character words, polysyllabic words (which have three or more characters) only take up a very small proportion; the rest are all dissyllabic words (two-character words).

To draw an analogy with English words, multi-character Chinese words are 'compound words', or 'compounds' in short. In most cases, Chinese compounds are very short, and individual characters are there to serve as semantic elements of the compounds.

9.2.1 Words containing homophonic and polyphonic characters

Compared with other languages, the Chinese language is very rich in homophones and polyphones. For example, **Xinhua Dictionary** of 1971 Edition has included 734 polyphones — 10% of all the characters collected.[2] Homophonic Chinese characters are different characters that share the same sound. A polyphonic Chinese character can have many different sounds (sometimes with only tone variations) to represent different meanings. Due to the ambiguous links between the sounds and meanings in homophonic and polyphonic characters, homophones and polyphones in Chinese present a particular challenge to the learners.

Examples of Homophonic Words

Example 1: 不详 and 不祥 (bùxiáng)

不详	not clear; not in detail
不祥	ominous; inauspicious

Example 2: 度过 and 渡过 (dùguò)

度过	to spend a period of time
渡过	to cross (a river etc.); to fly across

Words Containing Homophones That Have the Same Sound of 'cái'

Homophonic Character	Word	Pinyin	Meaning
才	才干	**cái**gàn	ability; competence
	刚才	gāng**cái**	just now; a moment ago
材	木材	mù**cái**	wood; timber
	材料	**cái**liào	material
财	财产	**cái**chǎn	property
	财富	**cái**fù	wealth; fortune
裁	裁员	**cái**yuán	layoff; downsize
	裁判	**cái**pàn	referee; judgement

Examples of Words Containing Polyphones

Example 1: 膀 (bǎng, páng)

翅膀	chì**bǎng**	wing
膀胱	**páng**huāng	bladder

Example 2: 会 (huì, kuài)

大会	dà**huì**	conference; mass meeting
会计	**kuài**jì	accounting; bookkeeper

Example 3: 差 (chā, chāi)

误差	wù**chā**	error
公差	gōng**chāi**	public errand

Example 4: 大 (*dà, dài*)

大小	*dà**xiǎo**	big or small
大夫	*dài**fu**	doctor

Example 5: 便 (*pián, biàn*)

便宜	*pián**yi**	cheap
方便	*fāng**biàn**	convenient

Example 6: 和 (*hé, hè, huó, huò, hú*)

和平	*hé**píng**	peace
和诗	*hè**shī**	compose a poem in reply
和面	*huó**miàn**	knead dough
和稀泥	*huò**xīní**	try to smooth things over
和了	*hú**le**	have won a set in a Mahjong game

9.2.2 Words translated from their foreign equivalents

Every language 'borrows' words from other languages. In the case of Chinese, when foreign words have to be imported into the native ones, depending on the nature of the words to be imported, new words would be created by adopting the following different approaches:
- to directly imitate the sounds
- to simply translate the meanings
- to creatively re-invent new words
- to combine all three

Examples of 'Foreign' Words

1) words created by imitating sounds

Chinese	坦克	吉普	扑克	蒙太奇
Pinyin	*tǎnkè*	*jípǔ*	*púkè*	*méngtàiqí*
English	tank	jeep	poker	montage

2) words created by re-inventing

Chinese	科学	哲学	资本	股票
Pinyin	*kēxué*	*zhéxué*	*zīběn*	*gǔpiào*
English	science	philosophy	capital	stock

3) words created by mixing different approaches

Chinese	芭蕾舞	迷你裙	保龄球
Pinyin	*bāléiwǔ*	*mínǐqún*	*bǎolíngqiú*
English	ballet	miniskirt	bowling

芭蕾舞 is the Chinese word for ballet, and it contains three *hanzi*:
- The first two characters 芭蕾 imitate the sound of 'ballet'.
- The last character 舞 is the Chinese word for dance.
- The addition of the Chinese character 舞 is very effective and customary, as in Chinese the name for any kind of dance normally ends with this character.

迷你裙 is the Chinese word for miniskirt, and it contains three *hanzi*:
- The first two characters 迷你 are pronounced exactly like 'mini', and mean 'to attract you' and 'to be attractive to you'.
- The last character 裙 is a direct translation of the word 'skirt'.

保龄球 is the Chinese word for bowling, and it contains three *hanzi*:
- The first two characters 保龄 imitate the sound of 'bowling', and mean 'to keep young', 'to stop aging' and 'to be fit and healthy' in Chinese.
- The last character 球 means ball.

4) examples of information technology related words
With the ever increasing widespread use of computers and the Internet globally, new words from information technology are no longer jargon for techies, but are becoming very popular in our daily life. When these new words are imported into Chinese, sometimes a few different Chinese words (for the same English term) are created and used in mix. This phenomenon of synonyms derived from technological advances and 'foreign' words is very natural in any language.

The table below presents some information technology related words and their Chinese equivalents.

English	Chinese & *Pinyin*
computer	计算机 (*jīsuànjī*), 电脑 (*diànnǎo*)
Internet	因特网 (*yīntèwǎng*), 互联网 (*hùliánwǎng*)
WWW	万维网 (*wànwéiwǎng*)

Intranet	内联网 (*nèiliánwǎng*),
	企业内部网 (*qǐyè nèibùwǎng*)
Extranet	外联网 (*wàiliánwǎng*),
	企业外部网 (*qǐyè wàibùwǎng*)
blog, weblog	网记 (*wǎngjì*), 博客 (*bókè*), 部落格 (*bùluògé*)
hacker	黑客 (*hēikè*)
router	路由器 (*lùyóuqì*)

9.3 Idioms and Proverbs

Every language has its own idioms and proverbs, which not only form a very important part of the language but also make up a considerable amount of the expressions used in daily conversation.

Sometimes it is very hard to strictly differentiate idioms, phrases, proverbs and sayings. ***Oxford Advanced Learner's Dictionary of Current English***[3] has the following two entries:

idiom — a phrase or sentence whose meaning is not clear from the meaning of its individual words and which must be learnt as a whole unit

proverb — a short well-known sentence or phrase that states a general truth about life or gives advice

Examples of English idioms include "Achilles' heel" (means *area of weakness*), and "give a hand" (means *help*). Examples of English proverbs include "you can't see the wood for the trees" and "you can lead the horse to water, but you can't make it drink."

In Chinese, correspondingly, there are '成语' (*chéngyǔ*) and '谚语' (*yànyǔ*):

成语 — Chinese idioms

谚语 — Chinese proverbs and sayings

In English, for idioms such as "give a hand" and "do or die", one can learn and understand them very easily; but for other idioms such as "Achilles' heel" and "meet one's Waterloo", one has to know their origins to fully appreciate their meanings. Similarly, in Chinese, for idioms such as 喜新厌旧 (means *love the new and loathe the old*) and 无可奈何 (means *have no alternative*), they can be learnt and understood easily; for idioms such as 刻舟求剑 and

掩耳盗铃, which will be discussed in detail later, one needs to know their origins to fully understand and use them.

9.3.1 idioms

The examples of Chinese idioms in this section will only include those which, to be fully appreciated, must be learnt by understanding their origins.

For each of the Chinese idioms presented below, the story of its origin will be briefly introduced.

1) 掩耳盗铃 (*yǎněr-dàolíng*)
Decomposition: the four characters and their meanings in the idiom are:

掩 (*yǎn*) — to cover (with the hand); shut, conceal; hide
耳 (*ěr*) — ear
盗 (*dào*) — rob, steal; thief
铃 (*líng*) — bell

Tone variation:

Literal translation: to steal the bell with both ears covered

The story in brief:
This is a story from ***Mister Lü's Spring and Autumn Annals***.[4]
This is set during the Spring and Autumn Period of China. A thief noticed a huge and beautiful bronze bell in the forecourt of a rich family. As he could not move it, he decided to break it into pieces with his hammer. Fearing the family would be woken by the striking sound, he came up with a 'clever' idea and stuffed two cloth rolls into his ears.

Meaning: to act/behave in a concealing way that only deceives oneself

2) 疑邻偷斧 (*yílín-tōufǔ*)

Decomposition: the four characters and their meanings in the idiom are:

疑 (*yí*) — doubt, suspect, question
邻 (*lín*) — neighbour
偷 (*tōu*) — steal, pilfer, hook
斧 (*fǔ*) — axe

Tone variation:

Literal translation: to be suspicious that the neighbour stole the axe

The story in brief:
This is a story from ***Liezi***.[5]

A man needed to use his axe, but just could not find it. Without any evidence, he immediately presumed that it was the son of his neighbour who stole it. From then on, he began to watch the boy, and noticed that everything the boy did — from the expression when the boy talked to the way the boy walked — seemed to suggest that the boy did steal the axe. One day, after a while, he unexpectedly found his axe somewhere completely overlooked, and suddenly remembered that he had done some work there before he thought he had lost his axe. Now, observing the boy again, he could not find anything unusual.

Meaning: to look at/think of things in prejudicial ways

3) 刻舟求剑 (*kèzhōu-qiújiàn*)
Decomposition: the four characters and their meanings in the idiom are:

刻 (*kè*) — carve, engrave
舟 (*zhōu*) — boat, ship
求 (*qiú*) — seek; beg
剑 (*jiàn*) — sword

Tone variation:

Literal translation: to carve the boat in order to get the sword back

The story in brief:
This is another story from *Mister Lü's Spring and Autumn Annals*.[6]
    While crossing a river on a boat, a man accidentally dropped his sword into the river. In hoping to get the sword back, at the location where the sword sank, he carved a mark onto the boat. As soon as the boat reached the other side of the river, he paid a good swimmer to dive into the river from the marked location to try to find his sword. Not surprisingly, despite all the efforts of the swimmer, the sword just could not be found.

Meaning: to lack the realization that things are changing rapidly, but to view things statically and in isolation

4) 守株待兔 (*shǒuzhū-dàitù*)
Decomposition: the four characters and their meanings in the idiom are:
    守 (*shǒu*) — defend, guard, observe
    株 (*zhū*) — individual plant; stump
    待 (*dài*) — wait, treat, receive
    兔 (*tù*) — hare, rabbit

Literal translation: to stay by the stump and wait for more hares

Tone variation:

The story in brief:
This is a story from *Hanfeizi*.[7]
    Once, a scared hare dashed out of a bush, unfortunately bumped into a stump and died. A farmer working nearby on his

family farm saw what had happened, went home with the hare, and thought that his turn of fortune had finally arrived.

From then on, he no longer worked on the farm, but sat by the stump and waited for more hares. Days went by and although no more such 'good' things occurred, he did not want to give up and kept thinking "it would happen tomorrow."

Meaning: to dream for chances and windfalls without working hard for them; to be inflexible and take a one-off experience as a golden rule.

9.3.2 Proverbs and sayings

For some Chinese proverbs and sayings, there can be a few translations or equivalent English sayings.

1) 欲速则不达
Pinyin: *yùsù zé bùdá*

English translation/equivalent:
Haste does not bring success.
More haste, less speed.

2) 巧妇难为无米之炊
Pinyin: *qiǎofù nánwéi wúmǐ zhīchuī*

English translation/equivalent:
The cleverest housewife can't cook a dinner without rice.
You can't make an omelette without breaking eggs.
One can't make bricks without straw.

3) 知己知彼，百战不殆
Pinyin: *zhījǐ zhībǐ, bǎizhàn bùdài*

English translation/equivalent:
Know yourself and know the enemy; you will never be defeated in a hundred battles.
Know yourself, and know your enemy, a hundred battles, a hundred wins.

4) 一寸光阴一寸金, 寸金难买寸光阴
Pinyin: *yīcùn guāngyīn yīcùn jīn, cùn jīn nánmǎi cùn guāngyīn*

English translation/equivalent:
An inch of time is an inch of gold, but you can't buy an inch of time with an inch of gold.
Time is money.

5) 无风不起浪
Pinyin: *wúfēng bù qǐlàng*

English translation/equivalent:
No wind, no waves.
There is a reason for everything.
There's no smoke without fire.

6) 纸包不住火
Pinyin: *zhǐ bāobùzhù huǒ*

English translation/equivalent:
Paper can't wrap up a fire.
Truth will come to light sooner or later.

7) 千里之行始于足下
Pinyin: *qiānlǐ zhīxíng shǐyú zúxià*

English translation/equivalent:
A thousand-mile journey begins with the first step.

8) 当事者迷, 旁观者清
Pinyin: *dāngshìzhě mí, pángguānzhě qīng*

English translation/equivalent:
The participant's perspectives are clouded while the bystander's views are clear.

9) 不入虎穴, 焉得虎子
Pinyin: *bùrù hǔxué, yāndě hǔzǐ*

English translation/equivalent:
If you don't go into the cave of the tiger, how are you going to get its cub?
Nothing ventured, nothing gained.

10) 一朝被蛇咬，十年怕井绳
Pinyin: *yīzhāo bèi shéyǎo, shínián pà jǐngshéng*

English translation/equivalent:
A burnt child dreads fire.
Once bitten , twice shy.

11) 狗嘴吐不出象牙来
Pinyin: *gǒuzuǐ tù bùchū xiàngyá lái*

English translation/equivalent:
Elephant tusks cannot grow out of a dog's mouth.
A filthy mouth can't utter decent language.

12) 不识庐山真面目，只缘身在此山中
Pinyin: *bùshí lúshān zhēnmiànmù, zhǐyuán shēnzài cí shānzhōng*

English translation/equivalent:
You can't see the wood for the trees.

13) 车到山前必有路
Pinyin: *chē dào shānqián bì yǒulù*

English translation/equivalent:
Things will eventually sort themselves out.

14) 路遥知马力，日久见人心
Pinyin: *lùyáo zhī mǎlì, rìjiǔ jiàn rénxīn*

English translation/equivalent:
Distance tests a horse's strength; time reveals a person's heart.

15) 师傅领进门，修行在个人
Pinyin: *shīfu lǐng jìnmén, xiūxíng zài gèrén*

English translation/equivalent:
You can lead the horse to water, but you can't make it drink.

16) 说曹操，曹操到
Pinyin: *shuō cáocāo, cáocāo dào*

English translation/equivalent:
Talk of the devil, and he is sure to appear.

Hanzi Study (2): Chinese Character Riddles

10

汉字学习（二）：汉字谜

"The perfect use of language is that in which every word carries the meaning that it is intended to, no less and no more."

Cyril Connolly (*The Enemies of Promise*)

People all over the world love playing word games for the following reasons:

- The rules are simple, but the games can be challenging and inspirational.
- They can be a one-player game or a team activity.
- They cost little, but have many benefits.
- They can be played almost anywhere and any time.

Nowadays word games are played in all sorts of different ways and using different media — on newspapers, playing online, playing live on TV and radio, and playing on mobile phones etc.

In English, among its many varieties of word games, the crossword puzzle is probably the most common one. Crossword puzzles are essentially about containment and association, as in English, words are one-dimensional (that is, they are made up by putting phonetic characters together sequentially).

In Chinese, the character riddle is the most popular form of word game. As Chinese characters consist of components and strokes, and in most cases each character is a word itself, Chinese character riddles are about division, analysis and synthesis.

Playing Chinese character riddles is not only great fun but also an excellent way to learn and understand *hanzi*.

10.1 Sample Riddles

When trying to work out a *hanzi* riddle, the following tips will prove very helpful:
1) Read it through a few times and think it over;
2) See whether the riddle has explicitly indicated the structure of the character — be it left and right, top and bottom, inside and outside, etc.;
3) Try to keep your mind open and think laterally;
4) If you cannot find any clue in the original riddle, try to think whether the riddle can be re-phrased (without altering the meaning) literally. Example 7 presents a typical case;
5) Bear in mind that riddles can appear in various forms. Sometimes one sentence can include all the clues needed (as in example 1); sometimes each sentence corresponds to a specific part of the character (as in the case of example 4); at other times all the sentences relate to the character in question (as in example 14).

No	Original Riddle in Chinese	Translation	Answer in Chinese	Answer in English
1	顶着日头作业	to work while the sun is hanging over your head	显 *xiǎn*	show, display
2	第二次握手	to shake hands for the second time	观 *guān*	watch, see
3	鱼头蛇尾巴，成天满地爬	With the head of a fish (鱼) and the tail of a snake (蛇), it crawls on the ground all day long.	龟 *guī*	turtle
4	左边生鳞不生角，右边生角不生鳞	The left has got scales but no horns; the right has got horns but no scales.	鲜 *xiān*	fresh
5	天没有它大，人有它大	Without it, 天 becomes 大; with it, 人 reads 大.	一 *yī*	one

6	左看两点水，右看全是水。细看不是水，其实还是水。	Watching its left, you can see two drops of water; watching its right, you see nothing but water. Looking closely, it is not water; but in reality, it is water.	冰 *bīng*	ice
7	二姑娘	the second daughter	姿 *zī*	appearance, looks
8	门庭若市	The courtyard is as crowded as a marketplace.	闹 *nào*	noisy
9	一千零一夜	one thousand and one nights	歼 *qiān*	annihilate
10	左边加一是千，右边减一是千	Adding 一 (one) to the left makes 千; taking away 一 (one) from the right equals 千 as well.	任 *rèn*	appoint; let, allow
11	三人同日见，百花齐争艳	Three people meet on the same day, flowers blossom in a riot of colours.	春 *chūn*	spring
12	门上生翠竹，日光照门中	Green bamboos grow above the door, while the sun is shining inside.	简 *jiǎn*	simple
13	看起来圆又圆，写起来是九点	Looking at it, it is very round; writing it, it is a nine (九) and a dot (点).	丸 *wán*	ball
14	有水可以养鱼，有土可以种瓜；有人不是你我，有马走遍天下。	Adding water, fish could be bred in it; adding soil, melons could be grown on it; adding a person, it is neither you nor me; adding a horse, galloping across vast plains would be made easy.	也 *yě*	also, too

| 15 | 左边绿，右边红；右怕水，左怕虫。 | The left is green and the right is red; the right is afraid of water and the left is scared of insects. | 秋 qiū | autumn |
| 16 | 一人二人，治病救人 (两字) | One person and two people, their job is to take care of patients and rescue people. (Answer is in two characters.) | 大夫 dāifu | doctor |

10.2 Explanations

As it has been shown in previous chapters, the majority of Chinese characters are composed of two or more parts (components). This multi-component feature of *hanzi* is actually, in most cases, the source of Chinese character riddles.

| 1 | 顶着日头作业 | to work while the sun is hanging over your head | 显 xiǎn | show, display |

Analysis:
1) Literally, the riddle hints a top and bottom structure as 'the sun is hanging over the head'.
2) The top part is related to the sun, which in Chinese is 日.
3) The bottom part — 'to work' — seems tricky and subtle. 'To work' is actually the literal translation of the last two Chinese characters '作业' in the original riddle, from which we can come up with the Chinese characters 业, 干 and so on.
4) Think about the last two Chinese characters '作业' laterally. As the first character 作 has the same sound as the Chinese character '坐', which literally means 'sit', it is safe to assume that '作业' may imply '坐业'. In Chinese, '坐业' literally means that 业 is sitting there (under the sun 日 in this case).

Answer:
Based on the above analysis, the character 显 is the answer we are looking for.

| 2 | 第二次握手 | to shake hands for the second time | 观
guān | watch, see |

Analysis:
1) The riddle has not given any hint about the structure.
2) It is very difficult to directly associate a Chinese character with this riddle. Remember the tips that were mentioned earlier? Let us see whether the original riddle can be expressed in different ways.
3) 'To shake hands for the second time' — it implies 'see (you) again', or 'meet (you) again'. In Chinese, 'see/meet again' is '又见'. Combining the two characters 又 and 见 gives another character 观, which also means 'watch/see'.

Answer:
   From the above analysis, the character 观 is the character intended, and it fits the riddle both literally and metaphorically.

| 3 | 鱼头蛇尾巴，
成天满地爬 | With the head of a fish (鱼) and the tail of a snake (蛇), it crawls on the ground all day long. | 龟
guī | turtle |

Analysis:
1) The riddle has hinted a top and bottom structure.
2) The character in question represents an animal that crawls on the ground.
3) Literally, the riddle says that the character has got the head of the character 鱼 (fish) and the tail of the character 蛇 (snake). Looking at these two characters, it is not difficult to see that the top and bottom parts are '龟' and '乚', respectively.

Answer:
   The character 龟 is the character intended.

| 4 | 左边生鳞不生角，右边生角不生鳞 | The left has got scales but no horns; the right has got horns but no scales. | 鲜
xiān | fresh |

Analysis:
1) The riddle has hinted a left and right structure.

2) The left suggests something that has got scales but no horns, so fish fits. In Chinese, the character 鱼 is the general term for fish, and a lot of characters related to specific types of fish have got 鱼 as the pictographic part.
3) The right indicates something that has got horns but no scales, so it could be any animal with horns such as 羊 (goat), 牛 (ox), 鹿 (dear) etc.
4) The only combination from 2) and 3) that gives a Chinese character is 鲜, which consists of 鱼 and 羊 and fits the riddle very well.

Answer: 鲜

5	天没有它大， 人有它大	Without it, 天 becomes 大; with it, 人 reads 大.	一 *yī*	one

Analysis:
1) No structure has been indicated.
2) The English translation given comes from one of many ways to read the riddle (and is actually the intended way). The riddle can also be translated as "the sky is smaller than it; but man is bigger than it", which does not make much sense.
3) Taking away 一 (one) from 天 gives 大; adding 一 to 人 also gives 大.

Answer: 一

6	左看两点水， 右看全是水。 细看不是水， 其实还是水。	Watching its left, you can see two drops of water; watching its right, you see nothing but water. Looking closely, it is not water; but in reality, it is water.	冰 *bīng*	ice

Analysis:
1) The riddle consists of 4 sentences. The first two sentences obviously indicate that the character in question has a left and right structure.
2) From the first two sentences, you can come out with the

character 冰 straightaway.
3) The last two sentences obviously verify and support the answer.

Answer: 冰

7	二姑娘	the second daughter	姿 *zī*	appearance, looks

Analysis:
1) No structure has been specified at all.
2) At first, it seems you cannot get anything out of this riddle, therefore some lateral thinking is necessary here. Let us see if there is any other way to express '二姑娘' ('the second daughter'). For a Chinese speaker, the expression '次女' will come to mind easily, as it means the same thing — the second daughter. Putting these two characters together vertically will give another character 姿.

Answer: 姿

8	门庭若市	The courtyard is as crowded as a marketplace.	闹 *nào*	noisy

Analysis:
1) No structure has been hinted, but as soon as one sees the riddle, the word 闹 (noisy) would naturally come to mind.
2) The character 闹 consists of two characters — 门 (door) and 市 (market), which are exactly the first and last characters of the original 4-character Chinese riddle.

Answer: 闹.

9	一千零一夜	one thousand and one nights	歼 *qiān*	annihilate

Analysis:
1) There is no hint about the structure.
2) Although the riddle reminds you of ***A Thousand and One Nights***, it does not seem to lead anywhere at the first look.
3) As Chinese characters are normally composed of two or more components, let us see if we can spot any components

in the original riddle.

4) 夜 (night) is not commonly used as a component. Only 3 characters in **XinHua Dictionary** [1] have it as a component, but none of them fits the riddle. However, another Chinese character 夕 also means night, and it has many uses.

5) 千 (thousand) can be used as a component, and it also has many uses.

6) With the two characters 夕 and 千 at hand, the character 歼 should come to mind quite easily.

Answer: 歼 — it has got one 千 (thousand), one 夕 (night) and a single-stroke character 一 (one) on top of the character 夕. It is indeed 'one thousand and one nights'.

10	左边加一是千，右边减一是千	Adding 一 (one) to the left makes 千; taking away 一 (one) from the right equals 千 as well.	任 *rèn*	appoint; let, allow

Analysis:

1) The character has got a left and right structure.

2) Put two 千 characters together horizontally and then inverse the actions suggested in the riddle: take 一 (one) away from the character 千 on the left, and add 一 (one) to the character 千 on the right. The result is the character 任.

Answer: 任.

11	三人同日见，百花齐争艳	Three people meet on the same day, flowers blossom in a riot of colours.	春 *chūn*	spring

Analysis:

1) No structure has been hinted.

2) Although the first sentence does not seem to give much of a clue, the second sentence reminds you of spring — the season when flowers blossom in a riot of colours.

3) In Chinese, the character 春 means 'spring'. On closer inspection of 春, you can disassemble it into three different characters: 三 (three), 人 (people/person), and 日 (day; the sun).

Answer: 春 fits the riddle excellently.

12	门上生翠竹， 日光照门中	Green bamboos grow above the door, while the sun is shining inside.	简 *jiǎn*	simple

Analysis:
  1) The structure has actually been hinted in both sentences.
  2) The first sentence points to a top and bottom structure: the character 门 (door) is underneath bamboos. In Chinese, 竹 means bamboo.
  3) The second sentence indicates the character 日 (the sun) is sitting inside the character 门.

Answer: 简 is the character in question, which consists of 竹, 门 and 日.

13	看起来圆又 圆，写起来是 九点	Looking at it, it is very round; writing it, it is a nine (九) and a dot (点).	丸 *wán*	ball

Analysis:
  1) The first sentence does not indicate the structure of the character in question, as all Chinese characters, except for the character 'O' (zero), are square-shaped. Therefore it seems to suggest the shape of the object that the character represents.
  2) The second sentence is actually about the structure, and the English translation given above only corresponds to one way of reading it — the intended one. In the original Chinese riddle, it says the character is made of '九点' — which can be interpreted in different ways: 1) nine dots; 2) 九 and 点; 3) 九 (nine) and '丶' (dot).

Answer: 丸 (ball) — it looks round and consists of 九 (nine) and '丶' (dot).

| 14 | 有水可以养鱼，有土可以种瓜；有人不是你我，有马走遍天下。 | Adding water, fish could be bred in it; adding soil, melons could be grown on it; adding a person, it is neither you nor me; adding a horse, galloping across vast plains would be made easy. | 也 yě | also, too |

Analysis:
1) Although no structure has been specified, each of the four sentences gives rise to one particular character, so it can be seen that the character in question is a quite popular character-component.
2) Let us firstly see what characters we can come up with from the four sentences. The first sentence reminds us of 池 (pond), 缸 (glass container); the second reminds us of 田 (field), 地 (land); the third reminds us of 他 (him) or 她 (her); the fourth reminds us of 驰 (gallop), 马车 (carriage).

Answer: 也. Adding '氵' (short form for water) to it gives the character 池 (pond); adding 土 (soil) to it gives 地 (land); adding '亻' (person) to it gives 他 (him); adding 马 (horse) to it gives 驰 (gallop).

| 15 | 左边绿，右边红；右怕水，左怕虫。 | The left is green and the right is red; the right is afraid of water and the left is scared of insects. | 秋 qiū | autumn |

Analysis:
1) A left and right structure has been clearly specified.
2) The left part is green and scared of insects — this indicates something to do with plants or leaves. This could be 禾 (shoots, as in bamboo shoots or rice shoots), which is actually a very popular character component.
3) The right part is red and afraid of water — this reminds us of 火 (fire).

Answer: 秋 fits all four hints. Further more, it is in autumn/fall (秋) that we get the mixture of green and red in nature.

16	一人二人，治病救人 (两字)	One person and two people, their job is to take care of patients and rescue people. (Answer is in two characters.)	大夫 *dāifu*	doctor

Analysis:

1) This is a riddle that asks for two characters. No structure has been specified for any of the characters in question.

2) The first sentence does not make any apparent sense, but the second one reminds us of doctors (医生, 大夫), nurses (护士) and hospitals (医院).

3) With these four words (医生, 大夫, 护士 and 医院) at hand, the first sentence in the riddle suddenly makes sense — it implies 大夫. The character 大 consists of two characters 一 (one) and 人 (person); the character 夫 consists of 二 (two) and 人 (person).

Answer: 大夫.

Appendix I

Current Frequently Used Chinese Characters
现代汉语常用字表

(a) 2500 most frequently used characters (常用字)

1 stroke (一画) — 2 words

一 乙

2 strokes (二画) — 17 words

二 十 丁 厂 七 卜 人 入 八 九 几 儿 了 力 乃 刀 又

3 strokes (三画) — 50 words

三 于 干 亏 士 工 土 才 寸 下 大 丈 与 万 上 小 口 巾 山 千 乞 川
亿 个 勺 久 凡 及 夕 丸 么 广 亡 门 义 之 尸 弓 己 已 子 卫 也 女
飞 刃 习 叉 马 乡

4 strokes (四画) — 105 words

丰 王 井 开 夫 天 无 元 专 云 扎 艺 木 五 支 厅 不 太 犬 区 历 尤
友 匹 车 巨 牙 屯 比 互 切 瓦 止 少 日 中 冈 贝 内 水 见 午 牛 手
毛 气 升 长 仁 什 片 仆 化 仇 币 仍 仅 斤 爪 反 介 父 从 今 凶 分
乏 公 仓 月 氏 勿 欠 风 丹 匀 乌 凤 勾 文 六 方 火 为 斗 忆 订 计
户 认 心 尺 引 丑 巴 孔 队 办 以 允 予 劝 双 书 幻

5 strokes (五画) — 137 words

玉 刊 示 末 未 击 打 巧 正 扑 扒 功 扔 去 甘 世 古 节 本 术 可 丙
左 厉 右 石 布 龙 平 灭 轧 东 卡 北 占 业 旧 帅 归 且 旦 目 叶 甲
申 叮 电 号 田 由 史 只 央 兄 叼 叫 另 叨 叹 四 生 失 禾 丘 付 仗
代 仙 们 仪 白 仔 他 斥 瓜 乎 丛 令 用 甩 印 乐 句 匆 册 犯 外 处
冬 鸟 务 包 饥 主 市 立 闪 兰 半 汁 汇 头 汉 宁 穴 它 讨 写 让 礼
训 必 议 讯 记 永 司 尼 民 出 辽 奶 奴 加 召 皮 边 发 孕 圣 对 台
矛 纠 母 幼 丝

6 strokes (六画) — 216 words

式 刑 动 扛 寺 吉 扣 考 托 老 执 巩 圾 扩 扫 地 扬 场 耳 共 芒 亚
芝 朽 朴 机 权 过 臣 再 协 西 压 厌 在 有 百 存 而 页 匠 夸 夺 灰
达 列 死 成 夹 轨 邪 划 迈 毕 至 此 贞 师 尘 尖 劣 光 当 早 吐 吓
虫 曲 团 同 吊 吃 因 吸 吗 屿 帆 岁 回 岂 刚 则 肉 网 年 朱 先 丢
舌 竹 迁 乔 伟 传 乒 乓 休 伍 伏 优 伐 延 件 任 伤 价 份 华 仰 仿
伙 伪 自 血 向 似 后 行 舟 全 会 杀 合 兆 企 众 爷 伞 创 肌 朵 杂
危 旬 旨 负 各 名 多 争 色 壮 冲 冰 庄 庆 亦 刘 齐 交 次 衣 产 决
充 妄 闭 问 闯 羊 并 关 米 灯 州 汗 污 江 池 汤 忙 兴 宇 守 宅 字

安讲军许论农讽设访寻那迅尽导异孙阵阳收阶阴防
奸如妇好她妈戏羽观欢买红纤级约纪驰巡

7 strokes (七画) — 264 words

寿弄麦形进戒吞远违运扶抚坛技环扰拒找批扯址走
抄坝贡攻赤折抓扮抢孝均抛投坟抗坑坊抖护壳志扭
块声把报却劫芽花芹芬苍芳严芦劳克苏杆杠杜材村
杏极李杨求更束豆两丽医辰励否还歼来连步坚早盯
呈时吴助县里呆园旷围呀吨足邮男困吵串员听吩吹
呜吧吼别岗帐财针钉告我乱利秃秀私每兵估体何但
伸作伯伶佣低你住位伴身皂佛近彻役返余希坐谷妥
含邻岔肝肚肠龟免狂犹角删条卵岛迎饭饮系言冻状
亩况床库疗应冷这序辛弃冶忘闲间闷判灶灿弟汪沙
汽沃泛沟没沈沉怀忧快完宋宏牢究穷灾良证启评补
初社识诉诊词译君灵即层尿尾迟局改张忌际陆阿陈
阻附妙妖妨努忍劲鸡驱纯纱纳纲驳纵纷纸纹纺驴纽

8 strokes (八画) — 310 words

奉玩环武青责现表规抹拢拔拣担坦押抽拐拖拍者顶
拆拥抵拘势抱垃拉拦拌幸招坡披拨择抬其取苦若茂
苹苗英范直茄茎茅林枝杯柜析板松枪构杰述枕丧或
画卧事刺枣雨卖矿码厕奔奇奋态欧垄妻轰顷转斩轮
软到非叔肯齿些虎虏肾贤尚旺具果味昆国昌畅明易
昂典固忠咐呼鸣咏呢岸岩帖罗帜岭凯败贩购图钓制
知垂牧物乖刮秆和季委佳侍供使例版侄侦侧凭侨佩
货依的迫质欣征往爬彼径所舍金命斧爸采受乳贪念
贫肤肺肢肿胀朋股肥服胁周昏鱼兔狐忽狗备饰饱饲
变京享店夜庙府底剂郊废净盲放刻育闸闹郑券卷单
炒炊炕炎炉沫浅法泄河沾泪油泊沿泡注泻泳泥沸波
泼泽治怖性怕怜怪学宝宗定宜审宙官空帘实试郎诗
肩房诚衬衫视话诞询该详建肃录隶居届刷屈弦承孟
孤陕降限妹姑姐姓始驾参艰线练组细驶织终驻驼绍
经贯

9 strokes (九画) — 316 words

奏春帮珍玻毒型挂封持项垮挎城挠政赴赵挡挺括拴
拾挑指垫挣挤拼挖按挥挪某甚革荐巷带草茧茶荒茫
荡荣故胡南药标枯柄栋相查柏柳柱柿栏树要咸威歪
研砖厘厚砌砍面耐耍牵残殃轻鸦皆背战点临览竖省
削尝是盼眨哄显哑冒映星昨畏趴胃贵界虹虾蚁思蚂
虽品咽骂哗咱响哈咬咳哪炭峡罚贱贴骨钞钟钢钥钩

卸 缸 拜 看 矩 怎 牲 选 适 秒 香 种 秋 科 重 复 竿 段 便 俩 贷 顺
修 保 促 侮 俭 俗 俘 信 皇 泉 鬼 侵 追 俊 盾 待 律 很 须 叙 剑 逃
食 盆 胆 胜 胞 胖 脉 勉 狭 狮 独 狡 狱 狠 贸 怨 急 饶 蚀 饺 饼 弯
将 奖 哀 亭 亮 度 迹 庭 疮 疯 疫 疤 姿 亲 音 帝 施 闻 阀 阁 差 养
美 姜 叛 送 类 迷 前 首 逆 总 炼 炸 炮 烂 剃 洁 洪 洒 浇 浊 洞 测
洗 活 派 洽 染 济 洋 洲 浑 浓 津 恒 恢 恰 恼 恨 举 觉 宣 室 宫 宪
突 穿 窃 客 冠 语 扁 袄 祖 神 祝 误 诱 说 诵 垦 退 既 屋 昼 费 陡
眉 孩 除 险 院 娃 姥 姨 姻 娇 怒 架 贺 盈 勇 怠 柔 垒 绑 绒 结 绕
骄 绘 给 络 骆 绝 绞 统

10 strokes (十画) — 284 words

耕 耗 艳 泰 珠 班 素 蚕 顽 盏 匪 捞 栽 捕 振 载 赶 起 盐 捎 捏 埋
捉 捆 捐 损 都 哲 逝 捡 换 挽 热 恐 壶 挨 耻 耽 恭 莲 莫 荷 获 晋
恶 真 框 桂 档 桐 株 桥 桃 格 校 核 样 根 索 哥 速 逗 栗 配 翅 辱
唇 夏 础 破 原 套 逐 烈 殊 顾 轿 较 顿 毙 致 柴 桌 虑 监 紧 党 晒
眠 晓 鸭 晃 晌 晕 蚊 哨 哭 恩 唤 啊 唉 罢 峰 圆 贼 贿 钱 钳 钻 铁
铃 铅 缺 氧 特 牺 造 乘 敌 秤 租 积 秧 秩 称 秘 透 笔 笑 笋 债 借
值 倚 倾 倒 倘 俱 倡 候 俯 倍 倦 健 臭 射 躬 息 徒 徐 舰 舱 般 航
途 拿 爹 爱 颂 翁 脆 脂 胸 胳 脏 胶 脑 狸 狼 逢 留 皱 饿 恋 桨 浆
衰 高 席 准 座 脊 症 病 疾 疼 疲 效 离 唐 资 凉 站 剖 竞 部 旁 旅
畜 阅 羞 瓶 拳 粉 料 益 兼 烤 烘 烦 烧 烛 烟 递 涛 浙 涝 酒 涉 消
浩 海 涂 浴 浮 流 润 浪 浸 涨 烫 涌 悟 悄 悔 悦 害 宽 家 宵 宴 宾
窄 容 宰 案 请 朗 诸 读 扇 袜 袖 袍 被 祥 课 谁 调 冤 谅 谈 谊 剥
恳 展 剧 屑 弱 陵 陶 陷 陪 娱 娘 通 能 难 预 桑 绢 绣 验 继

11 strokes (十一画) — 209 words

球 理 捧 堵 描 域 掩 捷 排 掉 堆 推 掀 授 教 掏 掠 培 接 控 探 据
掘 职 基 著 勒 黄 萌 萝 菌 菜 萄 菊 萍 菠 营 械 梦 梢 梅 检 梳 梯
桶 救 副 票 戚 爽 聋 袭 盛 雪 辅 辆 虚 雀 堂 常 匙 晨 睁 眯 眼 悬
野 啦 晚 啄 距 跃 略 蛇 累 唱 患 唯 崖 崭 崇 圈 铜 铲 银 甜 梨 犁
移 笨 笼 笛 符 第 敏 做 袋 悠 偿 偶 偷 您 售 停 偏 假 得 衔 盘 船
斜 盒 鸽 悉 欲 彩 领 脚 脖 脸 脱 象 够 猜 猪 猎 猫 猛 馅 馆 凑 减
毫 麻 痒 痕 廊 康 庸 鹿 盗 章 竟 商 族 旋 望 率 着 盖 粘 粗 粒 断
剪 兽 清 添 淋 淹 渠 渐 混 渔 淘 液 淡 深 婆 梁 渗 情 惜 惭 悼 惧
惕 惊 惨 惯 寇 寄 宿 窑 密 谋 谎 祸 谜 逮 敢 屠 弹 随 蛋 隆 隐 婚
婶 颈 绩 绪 续 骑 绳 维 绵 绸 绿

12 strokes (十二画) — 214 words

琴 斑 替 款 堪 搭 塔 越 趁 趋 超 提 堤 博 揭 喜 插 揪 搜 煮 援 裁
搁 搂 搅 握 揉 斯 期 欺 联 散 惹 葬 葛 董 葡 敬 葱 落 朝 辜 葵 棒
棋 植 森 椅 椒 棵 棍 棉 棚 棕 惠 惑 逼 厨 厦 硬 确 雁 殖 裂 雄 暂

雅 辈 悲 紫 辉 敞 赏 掌 晴 暑 最 量 喷 晶 喇 遇 喊 景 践 跌 跑 遗
蛙 蛛 蜓 喝 喂 喘 喉 幅 帽 赌 赔 黑 铸 铺 链 销 锁 锄 锅 锈 锋 锐
短 智 毯 鹅 剩 稍 程 稀 税 筐 等 筑 策 筛 筒 答 筋 筝 傲 傅 牌 堡
集 焦 傍 储 奥 街 惩 御 循 艇 舒 番 释 禽 腊 脾 腔 鲁 猾 猴 然 馋
装 蛮 就 痛 童 阔 善 羡 普 粪 尊 道 曾 焰 港 湖 渣 湿 温 渴 滑 湾
渡 游 滋 溉 愤 慌 惰 愧 愉 慨 割 寒 富 窜 窝 窗 遍 裕 裤 裙 谢 谣
谦 属 屡 强 粥 疏 隔 隙 絮 嫂 登 缎 缓 编 骗 缘

13 strokes (十三画) — 143 words
瑞 魂 肆 摄 摸 填 搏 塌 鼓 摆 携 搬 摇 搞 塘 摊 蒜 勤 鹊 蓝 墓 幕
蓬 蓄 蒙 蒸 献 禁 楚 想 槐 榆 楼 概 赖 酬 感 碍 碑 碎 碰 碗 碌 雷
零 雾 雹 输 督 龄 鉴 睛 睡 睬 鄙 愚 暖 盟 歇 暗 照 跨 跳 跪 路 跟
遣 蛾 蜂 嗓 置 罪 罩 错 锡 锣 锤 锦 键 锯 矮 辞 稠 愁 筹 签 简 毁
舅 鼠 催 傻 像 躲 微 愈 遥 腰 腥 腹 腾 腿 触 解 酱 痰 廉 新 韵 意
粮 数 煎 塑 慈 煤 煌 满 漠 源 滤 滥 滔 溪 溜 滚 滨 梁 滩 慎 誉 塞
谨 福 群 殿 辟 障 嫌 嫁 叠 缝 缠

14 strokes (十四画) — 88 words
静 碧 璃 墙 撤 嘉 摧 截 誓 境 摘 摔 聚 蔽 慕 暮 蔑 模 榴 榜 榨 歌
遭 酷 酿 酸 磁 愿 需 弊 裳 颗 嗽 蜻 蜡 蝇 蜘 赚 锹 锻 舞 稳 算 笋
管 僚 鼻 魄 貌 膜 膊 膀 鲜 疑 馒 裹 敲 豪 膏 遮 腐 瘦 辣 竭 端 旗
精 歉 熄 熔 漆 漂 漫 滴 演 漏 慢 寨 赛 察 蜜 谱 嫩 翠 熊 凳 骡 缩

15 strokes (十五画) — 64 words
慧 撕 撒 趣 趟 撑 播 撞 撤 增 聪 鞋 蕉 蔬 横 槽 樱 橡 飘 醋 醉 震
霉 瞒 题 暴 瞎 影 踢 踏 踩 踪 蝶 蝴 嘱 墨 镇 靠 稻 黎 稿 稼 箱 箭
篇 僵 躺 僻 德 艘 膝 膛 熟 摩 颜 毅 糊 遵 潜 潮 懂 额 慰 劈

16 strokes (十六画) — 36 words
操 燕 薯 薪 薄 颠 橘 整 融 醒 餐 嘴 蹄 器 赠 默 镜 赞 篮 邀 衡 膨
雕 磨 凝 辨 辩 糖 糕 燃 澡 激 懒 壁 避 缴

17 strokes (十七画) — 19 words
戴 擦 鞠 藏 霜 霞 瞧 蹈 螺 穗 繁 辫 赢 糟 糠 燥 臂 翼 骤

18 strokes (十八画) — 6 words
鞭 覆 蹦 镰 翻 鹰

19 strokes (十九画) — 7 words
警 攀 蹲 颤 瓣 爆 疆

20 strokes (二十画) — 8 words
壤 耀 躁 嚼 嚷 籍 魔 灌

21 strokes (二十一画) — 3 words
蠢 霸 露

22 strokes (二十二画) — 1 word
囊

23 strokes (二十三画) — 1 word
罐

(b) 1000 next most frequently used characters (次常用字)

2 strokes (二画) — 2 words
匕 刁

4 strokes (四画) — 8 words
丐 歹 戈 夭 仑 讥 冗 邓

5 strokes (五画) — 14 words
艾 夯 凸 卢 叭 叽 皿 凹 囚 矢 乍 尔 冯 玄

6 strokes (六画) — 34 words
邦 迂 邢 芋 芍 吏 夷 吁 吕 吆 屹 廷 迄 臼 仲 伦 伊 肋 旭 匈 凫 妆
亥 汛 讳 讶 讹 讼 诀 弛 阱 驮 驯 纫

7 strokes (七画) — 77 words
玖 玛 韧 抠 扼 汞 扳 抢 坎 坞 抑 拟 抒 芙 芜 苇 芥 芯 芭 杖 杉 巫
杈 甫 匣 轩 卤 肖 吱 吠 呕 呐 吟 呛 吻 吭 邑 囤 吮 岖 牡 佑 佃 伺
囱 肛 肘 甸 狈 鸠 彤 灸 刨 庇 吝 庐 闰 兑 灼 沐 沛 汰 沥 沧 汹 沧
沪 忱 诅 诈 罕 屁 坠 妓 姊 妒 纬

8 strokes (八画) — 97 words
玫 卦 坷 坯 拓 坪 坤 拄 拧 拂 拙 拇 拗 茉 昔 苛 苦 苟 苞 茁 苔 枉
枢 枚 枫 杭 郁 矾 奈 奄 殴 歧 卓 昙 哎 咕 呵 咙 呻 咒 咆 咖 帕 账
贬 贮 氛 秉 岳 侠 侥 侣 侈 卑 刽 刹 肴 觅 忿 瓮 肮 肪 狞 庞 疟 疙
疚 卒 氓 炬 沽 沮 泣 泞 泌 沼 怔 怯 宠 宛 衩 祈 诡 帚 屉 孤 弥 陋
陌 函 姆 虱 叁 绅 驹 绊 绎

9 strokes (九画) — 99 words
契 贰 玷 玲 珊 拭 拷 拱 挟 垢 垛 拯 荆 茸 茬 荚 茵 茴 荞 荠 荤 荧
荔 栈 柑 栅 柠 柳 勃 柬 砂 泵 砚 鸥 轴 韭 虐 昧 盹 咧 眨 昭 盅 勋
哆 咪 哟 幽 钙 钝 钠 钦 钧 钮 毡 氢 秕 俏 俄 俐 侯 徊 衍 胚 胧 胎
狰 饵 峦 奕 咨 飒 闺 闽 籽 娄 烁 炫 洼 柒 涎 洛 恃 恍 恬 恤 宦 诚
诓 祠 诲 屏 屎 逊 陨 姚 娜 蚤 骇

10 strokes (十画) — 107 words

耘 耙 秦 匿 埂 捂 捍 袁 捌 挫 挚 捣 捅 埃 耿 聂 莩 莽 莱 莉 莹 莺
梆 栖 桦 栓 桅 桩 贾 酌 砸 砟 砾 殉 逞 哮 唠 哺 剔 蚌 蚜 畔 蚣 蚪
蚓 哩 圃 鸯 唁 哼 唆 峭 唧 峻 赂 赃 钾 铆 氨 秣 笆 俺 赁 偶 殷 耸
臽 豺 豹 颁 胯 胰 脐 脓 逛 卿 鸵 鸳 馁 凌 凄 衰 郭 斋 疹 紊 瓷 羔
烙 浦 涡 涣 涤 涧 涕 涩 悍 悯 窍 诺 诽 袓 谆 崇 恕 娩 骏

11 strokes (十一画) — 142 words

琐 麸 琉 琅 措 捺 捶 赦 埠 捻 掐 掂 掀 掷 掸 掺 勘 聊 娶 菱 菲 萎
菩 萤 乾 萧 萨 菇 彬 梗 梧 梭 曹 酝 酗 厢 硅 硕 奢 盔 匾 颅 彪 眶
晤 曼 晦 冕 啡 畦 趾 啃 蛆 蚯 蛉 蛀 唬 啰 唾 啤 啥 啸 崎 逻 崔 崩
婴 赊 铐 铛 铝 铡 铣 铭 矫 秸 秽 笙 笤 偎 傀 躯 兜 舻 徘 徙 舶 舷
舵 敛 翎 脯 逸 凰 猖 祭 烹 庶 庵 痊 阎 阐 眷 焊 焕 鸿 淮 淑 淌 淮
淆 渊 淫 淳 淤 淀 涮 涵 惦 悴 惋 寂 窒 谍 谐 裆 袄 祷 谒 谓 谚 尉
堕 隅 婉 颇 绰 绷 综 绽 缀 巢

12 strokes (十二画) — 106 words

琳 琢 琼 揍 堰 揩 揽 揖 彭 揣 搀 搓 壹 搔 葫 募 蒋 蒂 韩 棱 椰 焚
椎 棺 椰 椭 粟 棘 酣 酥 硝 硫 颊 雳 翘 凿 棠 晰 鼎 喳 遏 晾 畴 跋
跛 蛔 蜒 蛤 鹃 喻 啼 喧 嵌 赋 赎 赐 锉 锌 甥 掰 氮 氯 黍 筏 牍 粤
逾 腌 腋 腕 猩 猬 惫 敦 痘 痢 痪 竣 翔 奠 遂 焙 滞 湘 渤 渺 溃 溅
湃 愕 惶 寓 窖 窘 雇 谤 犀 隘 媒 媚 婿 缅 缆 缔 缕 骚

13 strokes (十三画) — 89 words

瑟 鹉 瑰 搪 聘 斟 靴 靶 蓖 蒿 蒲 蓉 楔 椿 楷 榄 楞 楣 酪 碘 硼 碉
辐 辑 频 睹 睦 瞄 嗜 嗉 暇 畸 跷 踩 蜈 蜗 蜕 蛹 嗅 嗡 嗤 署 蜀 幌
锚 锥 锹 锭 锰 稚 颓 筷 魁 衙 腻 腮 腺 鹏 肄 猿 颖 煞 雏 馍 馏 廪
痹 廓 痴 靖 誉 漓 溢 溯 溶 滓 溺 寞 窥 窟 寝 裙 裸 谬 媳 嫉 缚 缤
剿

14 strokes (十四画) — 52 words

赘 熬 赫 蔫 摹 蔓 蔗 蔼 熙 蔚 兢 榛 榕 酵 碟 碴 碱 碳 辕 辖 雌 墅
喊 踊 蝉 嘀 幔 镀 舔 熏 箍 箕 箫 舆 僧 孵 瘩 瘟 彰 粹 漱 漩 漾 慷
寡 寥 谭 褐 褪 隧 嫡 缰

15 strokes (十五画) — 62 words

撵 撩 撮 撬 擒 墩 撰 鞍 蕊 蕴 樊 樟 橄 敷 豌 醇 磕 磅 碾 憋 嘶 嘲
嘹 蝠 蝎 蝌 蝗 蝙 嘿 幢 镊 镐 稽 篓 膘 鲤 鲫 褒 瘪 瘤 瘫 凛 澎 潭
潦 澳 潘 澈 澜 澄 憔 懊 憎 翩 褥 遣 鹤 憨 履 嬉 豫 缭

16 strokes (十六画) — 42 words

撼 擂 擅 蕾 薛 薇 擎 翰 噩 橱 橙 瓢 蟆 霍 霎 辙 冀 踱 蹂 蟆 螃 螟
噪 鹦 黔 穆 篡 篷 篙 篱 儒 膳 鲸 瘾 瘸 糙 燎 濒 懑 懈 窿 缱

17 strokes (十七画) — 32 words

壕 藐 檬 檐 檩 檀 礁 磷 瞭 瞬 瞳 瞪 曙 蹋 蟋 蟀 嚎 赡 镣 魏 簇 僮
徽 爵 朦 臊 鳄 糜 癌 懦 豁 臀

18 strokes (十八画) — 10 words

藕 藤 瞻 嚣 鳍 癞 瀑 襟 璧 戳

19 strokes (十九画) — 13 words

攒 孽 蘑 藻 鳖 蹭 蹬 簸 簿 蟹 靡 癣 羹

20 strokes (二十画) — 7 words

鬓 攘 蠕 巍 鳞 糯 譬

21 strokes (二十一画) — 3 words

霹 躏 髓

22 strokes (二十二画) — 3 words

蘸 镶 瓤

24 strokes (二十四画) — 1 words

矗

Appendix II

A Brief Chinese Chronology
中国历史年代简表

Xia (夏)			2070 – 1600 BC
Shang (商)			1600 – 1046 BC
Zhou (周)			1046 – 256 BC
	Western Zhou (西周)		1046 – 771 BC
	Eastern Zhou (东周)		770 – 256 BC
		Chun Qiu (Spring and Autumn Period) (春秋)	770 – 476 BC
		Zhan Guo (Warring States) (战国)	475 – 221 BC
Qin (秦)			221 – 206 BC
Han (汉)			206 BC – 220 AD †
	Western Han (西汉)		206 BC – 24
	Eastern Han (东汉)		25 – 220
San Guo (Three Kingdoms) (三国)			220 – 265
	Wei (魏)		220 – 265
	Shu (蜀)		221 – 263
	Wu (吴)		222 – 280
Western Jin (西晋)			265 – 316
Eastern Jin (东晋)			317 – 420
Sixteen Kingdoms (十六国)			304 – 439
Southern and Northern Dynasties (南北朝)			420 – 589
	Southern Dynasties (南朝)		
		Song (宋)	420 – 479
		Qi (齐)	479 – 502
		Liang (梁)	502 – 557
		Chen (陈)	557 – 589
	Northern Dynasties (北朝)		
		Northern Wei (北魏)	386 – 534
		Eastern Wei (东魏)	534 – 550
		Northern Qi (北齐)	550 – 577
		Western Wei (西魏)	535 – 557
		Northern Zhou (北周)	557 – 581

Dynasty	Subdivision	Dates
Sui (隋)		581 – 618
Tang (唐)		618 – 907
Five Dynasties and Ten Kingdoms (五代十国)	Later Liang (后梁)	907 – 923
	Later Tang (后唐)	923 – 936
	Later Jin (后晋)	936 – 946
	Later Han (后汉)	947 – 950
	Later Zhou (后周)	951 – 960
	Ten Kingdoms (十国)	902 – 979
Song (宋)	Northern Song (北宋)	960 – 1127
	Southern Song (南宋)	1127 – 1279
Liao (辽)		916 – 1125
West Xia (西夏)		1032 – 1227
Jin (Gold) (金)		1115 – 1234
Yuan (元)		1271 – 1368
Ming (明)		1368 – 1644
Qing (清)		1644 – 1911
Republic of China (中华民国)		1912 – 1949
People's Republic of China (中华人民共和国)		1949 –

† After the first appearance of an AD date, the letters 'AD' are omitted from the other AD dates.

Appendix III

ASCII Table
美国信息互换标准代码

ASCII, short for American Standard Code for Information Interchange, is a 7-bit encoding system. Please note that:
- All the characters within the shaded area are printable ASCII characters.
- The character code (in heximal) for each character is the combination of the column digit (0 – 7) with the row digit (0 – 9, A – F). For instance, the character code in heximal for character 'C' is 43 (which is equivalent to 67=16*4+3 in decimal); the character code in heximal for character 'm' is 6D (which is equivalent to 109=16*6+13 in decimal).

	0	1	2	3	4	5	6	7
0	NUL	DLE	space	0	@	P	`	p
1	SOH	DC1	!	1	A	Q	a	q
2	STX	DC2	"	2	B	R	b	r
3	ETX	DC3	#	3	C	S	c	s
4	EOT	DC4	$	4	D	T	d	t
5	ENQ	NAK	%	5	E	U	e	u
6	ACK	SYN	&	6	F	V	f	v
7	BEL	ETB	'	7	G	W	g	w
8	BS	CAN	(	8	H	X	h	x
9	HT	EM	)	9	I	Y	i	y
A	LF	SUB	*	:	J	Z	j	z
B	VT	ESC	+	;	K	[	k	{
C	FF	FS	,	<	L	\	l		
D	CR	GS	-	=	M	]	m	}
E	SO	RS	.	>	N	^	n	~
F	SI	US	/	?	O	_	o	DEL

References
参考文献

The following are the principal resources referred to in the book.

Chapter 1

1. 《人民日报》, 1956年1月31日。
   The People's Daily, January 31, 1956.
2. 吴浩坤, 潘悠, 《中国甲骨文史》, 上海人民出版社, 1985年, 上海。
   Wu Haokun, Pan You, *A History of Tortoise-Shell and Bone Inscriptions in China*, Shanghai People's Press, 1985, Shanghai.
3. [日] 阿辻哲次, 高文汉 译, 《图说汉字的历史》, 山东画报出版社, ISBN 7-80713-078-4, 2005年, 济南。
   The History of Chinese Characters in Pictures, 2005.
4. 《世本》, *c.* 235 BC – 228 BC。
   Shiben, c. 235 BC – 228 BC.
5. 《荀子》, *c.* 313 BC – 238 BC。
   Xunzi, c. 313 BC – 238 BC.
6. 《吕氏春秋》, *c.* 221 BC。
   Mister Lü's Spring and Autumn Annals, c. 221 BC.
7. 《韩非子》, *c.* 275 BC – 221 BC。
   Hanfeizi, c. 275 BC – 221 BC.
8. 许慎, 《说文解字》, *c.* 100 – 121 AD。
   Xu Shen, *Shuowen Jiezi* (*Explaining Simple and Analysing Compound Characters*), *c.* 100 – 121 AD.
9. 河南省文物考古研究所, 《舞阳贾湖》 (上卷), 科学出版社, ISBN 7-03-006923-4, 1999年, 北京。
   Jiahu of Wuyang, 1989.
10. Xueqin Li, Garman Harbottle, Juzhong Zhang, Changsui Wang, "The earliest writing? Sign use in the seventh millennium BC at Jiahu, Henan Province, China", pp31–45, No 295, *Antiquity* **77**, 2003.
11. 徐大力, "蚌埠双墩新石器遗址陶器刻划初论", 《文物研究》第五辑, 黄山书社, 1989年, 合肥。
    "Introduction to the Neolithic pottery incisions at Shuangdun, Banbu", 1989.
12. 西安半坡博物馆, 《西安半坡》, 文物出版社, 1982年, 北京。
    Bangpo of Xi'an, 1982.
13. 王树明, "谈陵阳河与大朱村出土的陶尊'文字'", 《山东史前文化论文集》, 齐鲁书社, 1986年, 济南。

"Grey pottery marks/symbols unearthed at Lingyang River and Dazhu Village", 1986.

14. 王蕴智，"远古符号综类摹萃"，《中原文物》，2003年第6期，第10–26页。
"A collection of traced ancient marks/symbols", 2003.

15. 中国科学院考古研究所洛阳发掘队，"河南偃师二里头遗址发掘简报"，《考古》，1965年第5期。
"A briefing on the excavation of the ruins at Erlitou, Yanshi, Henan Province", 1965.

16. 岳南，《考古中国 — 夏商周断代工程解密记》，海南出版社，ISBN 978-7-5443-2027-6, 2007年, 海口。
Notes on Xia-Shang-Zhou Chronology Project, 2007.

17. 司马迁，《史记》，c. 145 BC – 93 BC。
Sima Qian，*Records of the Grand Historian of China*，c. 145 BC – 93 BC.

18. 曹锦炎，沈建华，《甲骨文校释总集》（20卷），上海辞书出版社，ISBN 7532621294, 2006年, 上海。
The Verification and Interpretation of Oracle Bone Inscriptions, 20 Volumes, 2006.

19. 王守信，《甲骨学通论》，中国社会科学出版社，ISBN 7-5004-0329-1, 1989年, 北京。
Wang Shouxin, *An Introduction to the Study of Tortoise-Shell and Bone Inscriptions*, China Social Sciences Press, ISBN 7-5004-0329-1, 1989, Beijing.

20. Steven Roger Fischer, *A History of Writing*, Reaktion Books, ISBN 1861891679, 2004, London.

21. Andrew Robinson, *The Story of Writing*, Thames & Hudson, ISBN 0-500-28156-4, 1995, London.

22. 苏培成，《现代汉字学参考资料》第129页，北京大学出版社，ISBN 7-301-00281-5, 2001年, 北京。
Su Peicheng, *References of Study of Current Chinese Characters*, p.129, Beijing University Press, ISBN 7-301-00281-5, 2001, Beijing.

Chapter 2

1. National Bureau of Statistics of China (中华人民共和国国家统计局): http://www.stats.gov.cn/tjgb/rkpcgb/qgrkpcgb/t20060316_402310923.htm, last visited on 26th July 2007.

2. *Scheme of the Chinese Phonetic Alphabet* (汉语拼音方案): http://www.china-language.gov.cn/gfbz/shanghi/001.htm,

last visited on 26th July 2007.

3.   Sky Connection: http://www.skyconnecton.co.uk/.

Chapter 3

1.   国家语言文字工作委员会，《现代汉语通用字表》，1988年。
        Current Commonly Used Chinese Characters, 1988.

2.   《基础教学用现代汉语常用字部件规范》，www.china-language.gov.cn/doc/bujianbiao(20031113).pdf, 2003年。
        Modern Chinese Common Character Component Standard of Elementary Teaching, 2003.

3.   凌云主编，《通用字笔顺字典》，北京工业出版社，ISBN 7-5639-0609-6, 2000年，北京。
        Stroke Order Dictionary of Commonly Used Chinese Characters, 2000.

4.   陈原，《现代汉语定量分析》，上海教育出版社，1989年，上海。
        Quantitative Analysis of Current Chinese, 1989.

5.   路克修等，《现代小学识字写字教学》，语文出版社，ISBN 7-80126-887-3, 2002年，北京。
        The Teaching of Chinese Characters Reading and Writing in Current Primary Schools, 2002.

6.   陈仁凤，陈阿宝，"一千高频度汉字的解析及教学构想"，《语言文字应用》，1998年第1期，第42–51页。
        "Analysis and teaching proposal of 1000 high frequency Chinese characters", 1998.

Chapter 4

1.   李梵，《汉字的故事》第152页，中国档案出版社，ISBN 7-80166-093-5, 2001年，北京。
        Stories of Hanzi, 2001.

Chapter 5

1.   The National Library of China (中国国家图书馆): http://www.nlc.gov.cn/.

2.   *Limited and Unlimited Growth*: http://www.ugrad.math.ubc.ca/coursedoc/math100/notes/mordifeqs/logistic.html, last visited on 26th July 2007.

3.   苏培成，《现代汉字学参考资料》第54页。
        Su Peicheng, *References of Study of Current Chinese Characters*, p.54.

4. 苏培成，《现代汉字学参考资料》第55页。
    Su Peicheng, *References of Study of Current Chinese Characters*, p.55.
5. 孙曼均，"汉字应用水平测试用字的统计与分级"，《语言文字应用》，2004年第1期，第63－70页。
    "Statistics and classification of the characters used in the Competence Test of Chinese Characters", 2004.
6. 贾洪卫，董坚，徐锐，"计算机与'红学'研究综论"，《湖北大学学报》，1991年第1期，第30–34页。
    "Computer and the study of 'A Dream of Red Mansions'", 1991.
7. China National Language and Character Working Committee (中国语言文字网): http://www.china-language.gov.cn/gfbz/index.htm, last visited on 26th July 2007.
8. 苏培成，《现代汉字学参考资料》第240页。
    Su Peicheng, *References of Study of Current Chinese Characters*, p.240.
9. Claude E. Shannon, "Prediction and entropy of printed English", pp50–64, *The Bell System Technical Journal* **30**, 1951.
10. 苏培成，《现代汉字学参考资料》第44–47页。
    Su Peicheng, *References of Study of Current Chinese Characters*, pp44–47.
11. 刘源，《现代汉语常用词词频词典》，宇航出版社，ISBN 7-80034-302-2，1990年，北京。
    Liu Yuan, *Frequency Dictionary of Current Frequently Used Chinese Vocabularies*, Astronautic Publishing House, ISBN 7-80034-302-2, 1990, Beijing.
12. 张凯，"汉语构词基本字的统计分析"，《语言教学与研究》，1997年第1期，第42–51页。
    "Statistics and Analysis of Frequently Used and Vocabulary Forming Chinese Characters", 1997.
13. 北京语言学院语言教学研究所，《汉语词汇的统计与分析》，外语教学与研究出版社，1985年，北京。
    Research Institute of Language Teaching, Beijing Language College, *Statistics and Analysis of Chinese Vocabularies*, Foreign Language Teaching and Research Press, 1985, Beijing.
14. Bernard Allanic (安雄), "The 'missing link' in the teaching of Chinese characters as a foreign language", paper

presented at the International Interdisciplinary Conference on *Hanzi Renzhi — How Western Learners Discover the World of Written Chinese*, Germersheim, Germany, 2005. http://www.fask.uni-mainz.de/inst/chinesisch/hanzirenzhi_papers_allanic.htm, last visited on 1st July 2007.

Chapter 6

1. 小学生字典编写组，《新编小学生字典》，第2版，人民教育出版社，ISBN 7-107-11234-1，1995年，北京。
   The Newly Compiled Elementary Student Dictionary, 2nd Ed, People's Education Press, ISBN 7-107-11234-1, 1995, Beijing.
2. 北京外国语学院英语系，《汉英词典》，商务印书馆，1980年，北京。
   A Chinese-English Dictionary, The Commercial Press, 1980.
3. 《新华字典》，第7版，商务印书馆，ISBN 7-100-00042-4，1992年，北京。
   Xinhua Dictionary, 7th Ed, The Commercial Press, ISBN 7-100-00042-4, 1992, Beijing.
4. 张玉书 等，《康熙字典》，1716年。
   Kangxi Dictionary, 1716.
5. China National Language and Character Working Committee (中国语言文字网): http://www.china-language.gov.cn/doc/CYBJGF(20031209).doc, last visited on 30th September 2007.

Chapter 7

1. GB2312-80, *Chinese Coded Character Set for Information Interchange, Basic Set* (信息交换用汉字编码字符集基本集): http://www.china-language.gov.cn/gfbz/scanning/gfhbz/gfbz27.htm, last visited on 30th September 2007.
2. 《信息技术信息交换用汉字编码字符集基本集的扩充（GB 18030-2000）》，中国标准出版社，ISBN 7-900138-29-3，2003年，北京。
   Chinese Coded Characters Set for Information Interchange, Extension for the Basic Set (GB 18030-2000), Standards Press of China, ISBN 7-900138-29-3, 2003, Beijing.
3. The Unicode Consortium: http://unicode.org/, last visited on 28th May 2007.

4.   王码 (Wangma): http://www.wangma.com.cn/, last visited on 27th May 2007.

5.   朱邦復工作室 (Laboratory of Chu Bong-Foo): http://www.cbflabs.com/, last visited on 27th May 2007.

6.   商务印书馆, 王云五 (Wang Yunwu): http://www.cp.com.cn/ht/newsdetail.cfm?iCntno=1179, last visited on 27th May 2007.

Chapter 8

1.   李忠华,《英语人名词典》, 上海外语教育出版社, ISBN 7810804413, 2002年, 上海。
       Li Zhonghua, *A Dictionary of English Names*, Shanghai Foreign Education Press, ISBN 7810804413, 2002, Shanghai.

2.   《新英汉词典（增补本）》, 第2版, 上海译文出版社, ISBN 7-5327-0143-3, 1994年, 上海。
       A New English-Chinese Dictionary (*Enlarged and Updated*), 2nd Ed, Shanghai Translation Publishing House, ISBN 7-5327-0143-3, 1994, Shanghai.

3.   《大英汉词典》, 外语教学与研究出版社, ISBN 9787560007816, 1999年, 北京。
       Great English-Chinese Dictionary, Foreign Language Teaching and Research Press, ISBN 9787560007816, 1999, Beijing.

4.   http://www.astrazeneca.com/

5.   http://www.astrazeneca.com.cn/

6.   http://www.diy.com/

7.   http://www.bnq.com.cn/

8.   http://www.carrefour.com/

9.   http://www.carrefour.com.cn/

10.   http://www.cisco.com/

11.   http://www.cisco.com/global/CN/

12.   http://www.cocacola.com/

13.   http://www.coca-cola.com.cn/

14.   http://www.ericsson.com/

15.   http://www.ericsson.com.cn/

16.   http://www.google.com/

17.   http://www.google.cn/

18.   http://www.hp.com/

19.   http://welcome.hp.com/country/cn/zh/welcome.html

20. http://www.jnj.com/
21. http://www.jnj.com.cn/
22. http://www.microsoft.com/
23. http://www.microsoft.com/china/
24. http://www.motorola.com/
25. http://www.motorola.com.cn/
26. http://www.nestle.com/
27. http://www.nestle.com.cn/
28. http://www.nokia.com/
29. http://www.nokia.com.cn/
30. http://www.daimlerchrysler.com/
31. http://www.daimlerchrysler.com.cn/
32. http://www.canon.com/
33. http://www.canon.com.cn/
34. http://www.ikea.com/
35. http://www.ikea.com/ms/zh_CN/
36. http://www.titoni.com/
37. http://www.ets.org/

Chapter 9

1. *Gregorian-Lunar Calendar Conversion Table Year (1901-2100)*: http://www.hko.gov.hk/gts/time/conversion1_text.htm, last visited on 28th May 2007.
2. 苏培成,《现代汉字学参考资料》第199页。
   Su Peicheng, *References of Study of Current Chinese Characters*, p.199.
3. A S Hornby, *Oxford Advanced Learner's Dictionary of Current English*, Fifth Ed, Oxford University Press, ISBN 0-19-431421-9, 1995, Oxford.
4. 《吕氏春秋•自知》, *c.* 221 BC。
   Mister Lü's Spring and Autumn Annals, *c.* 221 BC.
5. 《列子•说符》, *c.* 770 BC – 221 BC。
   Liezi, *c.* 770 BC – 221 BC.
6. 《吕氏春秋•察今》, *c.* 221 BC。
   Mister Lü's Spring and Autumn Annals, *c.* 221 BC.
7. 《韩非子•五蠹》, *c.* 275 BC – 221 BC。
   Hanfeizi, *c.* 275 BC – 221 BC.

Chapter 10

1. 《新华字典》。
   Xinhua Dictionary.

Illustration Credits
图片出处

The author and publisher wish to acknowledge the following sources of illustrative material and/or permission to reproduce it, and apologize for any omissions or errors in the form of credits given. Corrections may be made in further printing.

All the calligraphy works that not specifically mentioned below are by *Wu Longwei*.

Figure 1.2 (*Jiahu*): Courtesy of *Henan* Institute of Archaeology.

Figure 1.3 (*Shuangdun*): see 1.11 in References.

Figure 1.4 (*Banpo*): Courtesy of the Museum of *Banpo, Xi'an*.

Figure 1.7 (*Yinxu*): adapted from http://www.yingbishufa.com/ldbt/0001.HTM.

Figure 1.8 (*Yinxu*): adapted from http://www.yingbishufa.com/ldbt/0002.HTM.

Figure 1.10 (*Dayu* tripod): Courtesy of the National Museum of China.

Figure 1.13 (*Cao Quan* Stele) and Figure 1.14 (*Xuanmi* Pagoda Stele): Courtesy of *Xi'an* Stele Forest Museum.

Figure 6.2 and Figure 6.3: pages from *The Newly Compiled Elementary Student Dictionary*.

Figure 1.5 (*Dawenkou*), Figure 1.6 (*Erlitou*), Figure 1.11 (Stone Drums), Figure 1.12 (Mt. *Yi* Stele), Figure 1.15 (*Lantingxu*) and Figure 1.16 (Four Ancient Poems): traced by *Wu Longwei*.

Glossary
词汇

ASCII: American Standard Code for Information Interchange — a 7-bit character set based on the Latin alphabet as used in modern English. See also **EBCDIC** and **Unicode**.

Associate compound: Also called compound indicative. One type of Chinese characters, in which each character is created by combining two or more characters (or their simplified form) to indicate a new meaning associated with the conjunction of the composing elements. See also **Ideographic character**, **Pictographic character**, **Pictophonetic character**.

Bagua: Meaning 'eight trigrams' literally, it is a fundamental philosophical concept in ancient China. Graphically, it is generally represented by an octagonal diagram with a unique trigram (consisting of '—' and/or '--') on each side.

Basic and elementary Chinese characters: The 120 Chinese characters compiled and recommended for Chinese learners in this book. Fully understanding these 120 characters at the beginning of Chinese learning, among other benefits, will enable the essence of Chinese characters to be registered in learners' minds quickly and firmly.

Big5: Big Five encoding — one of the encoding schemes for Chinese characters, and it is used only in Taiwan and Hong Kong. See also **GB18030** and **Unicode**.

Bit: Binary digIT — the smallest unit of storage on an electronic digital system which can only hold one of two values — 0 and 1. See also **Byte**.

Bronze inscriptions: The ancient Chinese inscriptions that were cast into or carved on bronze wares during, in particular, the period of the *Zhou* dynasty. See also **Oracle bone inscriptions**.

Bronze script: The system of characters used to cast/carve bronze inscriptions.

Byte: A unit of storage on an electronic digital system which consists of a sequence of 8 bits and is capable of holding any character in alphanumeric data. See also **Bit**.

Cang Jie: A legendary figure in ancient China who was claimed to have invented Chinese characters.

Cantonese: One of the Chinese dialects, spoken in *Guangzhou* (also known as Canton) and Hong Kong.

CCC: Complex Chinese Characters, mainly used in Taiwan and Hong Kong. See also **SCC**, **TCC**.

Character code: Within a character set, each character is encoded into a corresponding (binary) value — character code.

Character root: This term is specifically used in the keyboard (Chinese character) input methods that make use of the structural aspect of Chinese characters, e.g. *Wubi*. The majority of character roots actually belong to character components; they have been selected innovatively and systematically to enable Chinese characters be inputted into computers in as few keystrokes as possible. See also **Component of *hanzi***.

Character set: An encoding scheme in which each character is represented by a unique binary value. ASCII, EBCDIC, GB18030 and Unicode are only a few examples.

Character-component: All Chinese characters are made up of components. The components that are characters themselves are referred to as character-components. See also **Component of *hanzi***.

Chengyu: Chinese idioms are referred to as *chengyu* in *pinyin*.

Chinese calligraphy: An art unique to Asian cultures. It typically uses brushes to write Chinese characters. When it is applied in daily writing with pen and pencil, it is called Chinese pen calligraphy, and can also be called Chinese calligraphy for short.

CJK: A collective term for Chinese, Japanese and Korean. The term is mainly used in the internationalization of software and communications. See also **CJKV**.

CJKV: CJK plus Vietnamese. See also **CJK**.

Clerical script: Also called official *Han* script — an early Chinese script developed during the *Han* dynasty. Although the script was gradually replaced some 400 years later by regular script, as a style of handwriting in Chinese calligraphy, it is still very popular. See also **Cursive hand**, **Regular script**, **Running hand**, **Seal script**.

Common language: Also referred to as Mandarin, or *putonghua*, the official spoken language in the People's Republic of China.

Component of *hanzi*: The independent small units in Chinese characters. Nearly all components consist of multiple strokes. See also **Stroke**.

Compound indicative: Another name for associative compound.

Compound vowel: In the context of Chinese pronunciation, out of all the vowel sounds, except for the 6 simple vowels represented by single Latin characters, the rest are compound vowels represented by multiple Latin characters.

Culture: Also referred to as archaeological culture, it indicates a pattern of similar artifacts and features from a specific period and within a specific area.

Cursive hand: Also called grass script, a style of handwriting in Chinese calligraphy. It aims for the fastest speed of writing, allows the writer to break some rules when necessary, and emphasizes on connectedness, smoothness, simplicity and abstraction. See also **Clerical script**, **Regular script**, **Running hand**, **Seal script**.

Dialect: A regional variety of language distinguished by accent, grammar, or vocabulary, especially a variety of speech differing from the standard speech pattern of the culture in which it exists.

Dissyllabic word: A word that consists of two syllables, for instance the English word 'common'. As far as Chinese is concerned, a two-character word is a dissyllabic word. See also **Monosyllabic word** and **Polysyllabic word**.

Dissyllable: A dissyllabic word is also called a dissyllable.

Double *Pinyin*: One of the Chinese character input methods, derived from the *Pinyin* method. See also ***Pinyin* method**.

EBCDIC: Extended Binary Coded Decimal Interchange Code — an 8-bit character set used on IBM mainframe computers. See also **ASCII** and **Unicode**.

Encoding: For the information exchange and processing in computers, the process of mapping characters to numerical values is called encoding.

Etymological dictionary: A dictionary that studies the origins of words.

Final: When the term is used in the context of the pronunciation of Chinese characters, it normally implies the remaining sound of a Chinese character. Each Chinese character contains only one syllable, which generally consists of an 'initial' consonant and a 'final' — the rest of the syllable. See also **Initial**.

Font: A design for a set of glyphs representing the characters from some particular character sets in a specific style, size, weight, spacing etc.

Four Corner: A method that was originally invented for indexing Chinese characters in dictionaries. The method has been adopted and developed for inputting Chinese characters into computers.

Full *Pinyin*: One of the Chinese character input methods, derived from the *Pinyin* method. See also ***Pinyin* method**.

GB: Short for *Guobiao*.

GB18030: Short for GB18030-2000.

GB18030-2000: The mandated standard, in the People's Republic of China, for encoding Chinese characters. See also **GB2312**, **Big5** and **Unicode**.

GB2312: Short for GB2312-80.

GB2312-80: An encoding standard, in the People's Republic of China, for encoding Chinese characters before the adoption of GB18030. GB18030 maintains compatibility with GB2312. See also **GB18030**, **Big5** and **Unicode**.

Glyph: An image used in the graphical representation of a character.

Guobiao: Short for *Guojia Biaozhun* (National Standard) or, in the context of information technology, *Guojia Biaozhun Ma* (National Standard Encoding) in the People's Republic of China.

Hanzi: The pronunciation of 汉字 (Chinese characters) in *pinyin*, literally means Chinese characters.

Harmoniously arranged skeleton: The core of the structure of Chinese characters, and it serves as a basic guide for elegantly writing and rendering each Chinese character with all its strokes and components.

Homophone: See **Homophonic characters**.

Homophonic characters: Homophonic (Chinese) characters are different characters that share the same sound.

Homophony: In the Chinese writing system, the characteristic of homophonic characters.

Ideograph: See **Ideographic character**.

Ideographic character: Also called self-explanatory character. One type of Chinese characters, in which each character is derived from a pictorial symbolizing an idea or an abstract concept. See also **Associate compound**, **Pictographic character**,

Pictophonetic character.

Indexing component: A component in Chinese characters that has been selected to serve as an index in Chinese dictionaries — there are on average 200 indexing components in most Chinese dictionaries. See also **Radical**.

Initial: When the term is used in the context of the pronunciation of Chinese characters, it normally implies the beginning sound of a Chinese character. Each Chinese character contains only one syllable, which generally consists of an 'initial' consonant and a 'final' — the rest of the syllable. See also **Final**.

Input method: In the context of using Chinese characters in computing, it implies an approach and the corresponding program that allow users of western keyboards to enter Chinese characters.

Intonation: The variation of pitch in spoken language.

Kangxi **Dictionary**: As the standard dictionary in the 18th and 19th centuries and with a collection of 47035 characters, it is the most comprehensive dictionary among all the Chinese dictionaries before the 20th century. Today it is an indispensable reference tool for readers who read and study non-contemporary Chinese literature.

Latinization: See **Romanization**.

Literacy: The ability to read, write, speak, and understand words.

Logogram: A single fundamental unit in written language that represents a morpheme — a meaningful unit of language.

Logographic character: Characters of logogram. Chinese characters are logographic characters. See also **Phonemic character** and **Syllabic character**.

Mandarin: See Common language.

Monosyllabic word: A word that consists of a single syllable, for instance the English word 'dog'. As far as Chinese is concerned, each Chinese character is a word and contains only one syllable; therefore each Chinese character is a monosyllabic word. See also **Dissyllabic word** and **Polysyllabic word**.

Monosyllable: A monosyllabic word is also called a monosyllable.

Morpheme: A unit of language that cannot be divided into smaller meaningful parts. See also **Phoneme**, **Syllable**.

Most frequently used characters: In the Chinese writing system, although there are over 50000 characters, the number of characters in frequent use is actually significantly smaller and is roughly stable during any specific period of time. In 1988, the China National Language and Character Working Committee published 3500 current frequently used characters, which include 2500 most frequently used characters.

Multi-character word: The Chinese words that have two or more characters are referred to as multi-character words, because, in most cases, each Chinese character itself is a word. See also **Monosyllabic word**, **Dissyllabic word** and **Polysyllabic word**.

Multi-component character: Those Chinese characters that can be disassembled into two or more components.

Mutually explanatory character: Mutually explanatory characters normally have the same root, share the same semantic element, and are mutually explicable, but sound different.

Neolithic: Of or relating to the cultural period of the last part of the Stone Age, which is also referred to as New Stone Age.

Official *Han* script: See Clerical script.

Oracle bone inscriptions: The ancient Chinese inscriptions incised on ox scapulae and tortoise shells during the *Shang* dynasty. See also **Bronze inscriptions**.

Oracle bone script: The system of characters used to incise oracle bone inscriptions.

Phoneme: The smallest sound unit that affects the meaning of a word. See also **Morpheme, Syllable**.

Phonemic character: Characters that represent the phonemes of a language. The Latin alphabet consists of phonemic characters. See also **Logographic characters, Syllabic characters.**

Phonetic loan character: A phonetic loan character is borrowed from an existing character (on the basis of sound) to represent a different meaning.

Phonetic part: The component in a pictophonetic character that is adopted to give an indication of the sound of the composed character. See also **Semantic part**.

Phono-semantic compound: See **Pictophonetic character**.

Pictograph: See **Pictographic character**.

Pictographic character: One type of Chinese characters, in which each character is derived from a pictorial symbolizing an object. See also **Associate compound, Ideographic character, Pictophonetic character**.

Pictophonetic character: One type of Chinese characters, in which each character generally consists of two parts: a semantic element to indicate the meaning, and a phonetic element to hint the sound of the constructed character. See also **Associate compound, Ideographic character, Pictographic character**.

Pinyin: The official romanization of Mandarin in the People's Republic of China, which is recognized by the United Nations and ISO (ISO-7098).

Pinyin **method**: One of the Chinese character input methods by means of *pinyin*. The method is the easiest and most commonly used Chinese character input method at present, albeit it is not the fastest method.

Pitch: Highness or lowness of sound.

Polyphone: See **Polyphonic character**.

Polyphonic character: A (Chinese) character that sounds differently in different contexts.

Polysyllabic word: A word that consists of three or more syllables, for instance English word 'yesterday'. As far as Chinese is concerned, a multi-character (three or more Chinese characters) word is a polysyllabic word. See also **Monosyllabic word**, **Dissyllabic word**.

Putonghua: Common language is referred to as *putonghua* in *pinyin*.

Radical: Chinese indexing components are normally and conveniently referred to as radicals. See **Indexing component**.

Radical indexing: A Chinese character locating method (in a Chinese dictionary) that makes use of radicals.

Redundancy: In a language, the repetition of linguistic information either inherent in the structure of the language or through excessive wordiness.

Regular script: The Chinese script developed during the *Sui* dynasty and the *Tang* dynasty, it is the script used today for both SCC and CCC. See also **Clerical script**, **Cursive hand**, **Running hand**, **Seal script**.

Romanization: A system for representing words or language with the Roman alphabet. As far as Chinese is concerned, it implies using the Latin script to transcribe Chinese sounds. The official romanization system adopted in the People's Republic of China is *pinyin*, which is recognized by the United Nations and ISO as the standard romanization for Mandarin.

Running hand: A style of handwriting in Chinese calligraphy that lies between cursive hand and regular script — fast, flexible and rule binding. See also **Clerical script**, **Cursive hand**, **Regular script**, **Seal script**.

SCC: Simplified Chinese Characters. See also **CCC**, **TCC**.

Script: A particular system of writing.

Seal script: A very old Chinese script evolved from oracle bone script and bronze script, and it was replaced by clerical script from around 200 BC. However, as a style of handwriting in Chinese calligraphy, it is still in use today. See also **Clerical script**, **Cursive hand**, **Regular script**, **Running hand**.

Self-explanatory character: See **Ideographic character**.

Semantic part: The component in a pictophonetic character that is adopted to give an indication of the meaning of the composed character. See also **Phonetic part**.

Shanghainese: One of the Chinese dialects, spoken in Shanghai.

Shuowen Jiezi: Explaining Simple and Analysing Compound Characters — the first etymological dictionary of Chinese characters complied by *Xu Shen* between 100 AD and 121 AD.

Single-character word: See **Monosyllabic word**.

Single-component characters: The Chinese characters that cannot be dissembled into two or more components.

Soft sound: When a (Chinese) character is used to construct a multi-character word or within a phrase/sentence, sometimes it will lose its original tone and, hence, become a weak and short sound — soft sound. It is not an independent tone outside of the existing four tones in Chinese, but a special sound variation in the context of sound sequence of multiple syllables.

Stroke: The smallest unit in Chinese characters. See also **Component of *hanzi***.

Stroke count: The number of strokes in a Chinese character.

Stroke order principles: The set of rules by which Chinese characters should be rendered for the benefits of speed, smoothness and calligraphy effect.

Syllabic character: Characters that represent the syllables of a language. Japanese characters are syllabic characters. See also **Logographic characters**, **Phonemic characters**.

Syllable: A unit of speech consisting of a single sound formed by a vowel, diphthong, or syllabic consonant alone, or by any of these sounds preceded, followed, or surrounded by one or more consonants. See also **Morpheme**, **Phoneme**.

TCC: Traditional Chinese Characters, another name for complex Chinese characters. See also **CCC**, **SCC**.

Three-level hierarchy: The structure of Chinese characters is a three-level hierarchy — entirety, components and strokes, entirety being the core.

Tone: The use of pitch and intonation contour in a language to distinguish words. Standard spoken Chinese — Mandarin — has four tones.

Tone sign: The four signs — ‾ ´ ˇ ` — that are used to mark the four tones of high and level, rising, fall-rise, and falling of Mandarin.

Two-character word: See **Dissyllabic word.**

Unicode: The universal standard, maintained by the Unicode Consortium, for encoding characters in all the writing systems in the world. See also **Big5**, **GB18030**.

UTF-16: The Unicode Transformation Format that serializes a Unicode scalar value as a sequence of 16 bits of two bytes. See also **UTF-8**.

UTF-8: The Unicode Transformation Format that serializes a Unicode scalar value as a sequence of one to four bytes. See also **UTF-16**.

Wade-Giles system: An early and well known (especially in English-speaking countries) romanization system for the Chinese language. Now, except in Taiwan, it has been replaced by the *pinyin* system inside and outside of the People's Republic of China. See also ***Pinyin***.

Wubi: A keyboard input method for inputting Chinese characters into computers by means of character roots. See also **Character root**.

Yanyu: Chinese proverbs and sayings are referred to as *yanyu* in *pinyin*.

Yinxu: Ruins of *Yin* — the archaeological site, located near *Anyang* in *Henan* province of China and dated *c.* 1300–1046 BC, where a massive number of oracle bone inscription bearing artifacts have been unearthed.

Names and Terms in Chinese
名字及术语的中文对照

Anhui	安徽
Anyang	安阳
associative compounds	会意字
bagua	八卦
Bai Juyi	白居易
Bangbu	蚌埠
Banpo	半坡
Banpo pottery inscriptions	半坡陶器契刻符号
basic and elementary Chinese characters	基础入门字
big seal script	大篆
bronze script	金文, 钟鼎文
bronze ware	青铜器
Cang Jie	仓颉
Cangjie input method	仓颉输入法
Cao Quan Stele	曹全碑
Cao Xueqin	曹雪芹
Chan River	浐河
character root	字根
Characters Needed by Masses	《群众急需字》
Chen Pengnian	陈彭年
China	中国
Chinese	中文, 汉语
Chinese calligraphy	书法
Chinese character component	汉字部件
Chinese-English Dictionary	《汉英词典》
clerical script	隶书
complex Chinese characters (CCC)	繁体字
computer	计算机, 电脑
Confucian Analects	《论语》
Confucius	孔子
consonant	辅音
Current Commonly Used Chinese Characters	《现代汉语通用字表》
Current Frequently Used Chinese Characters	《现代汉语常用字表》
cursive hand	草书
Cyrillic alphabet	基里尔字母

Dawenkou culture	大汶口文化
Dayu tripod	大盂鼎
dictionary	字典
dissyllabic words	两音节词
Double *Pinyin* input method	双拼输入法
Dream of Red Mansions, a	《红楼梦》
Du Fu	杜甫
Eastern *Jin*	东晋
Egyptian hieroglyphics	古埃及圣书字
Encyclopedia Dictionary of the Chinese Language	《中文大辞典》
Erlitou	二里头
evolution	进化
final	韵母
Four Ancient Poems	古诗四帖
Four Corner input method	四角号码输入法
Frequency Dictionary of Current Frequently Used Chinese Vocabularies	《现代汉语常用词词频词典》
Full *Pinyin* input method	全拼输入法
Great China Dictionary	《中华大字典》
Great Dictionary of Chinese Characters	《汉语大字典》
Gu Yewang	顾野王
Guangyun	《广韵》
Guobiao	国标
Guojia Biaozhun	国家标准
Guojia Biaozhun Ma	国家标准码
Han dynasty	汉朝
Hanfeizi	韩非子
hanzi	汉字
harmoniously arranged skeleton	间架结构
Henan	河南
high frequency *hanzi*	高频度汉字
homophones	同音字
homophony	同音
Hundred Family Names	《百家姓》
ideographic characters	指事字

idioms	成语
Indus valley script	印度河谷文字
initial	声母
Internet	因特网，互联网
Jiahu	贾湖
Jijiupian	《急就篇》
***Kangxi* Dictionary**	《康熙字典》
knotted cords	结绳
Lantingxu	兰亭序
Li Bai	李白
Liezi	列子
Linear A, Linear B	线形文字
Liu Gongquan	柳公权
logographic characters	语素文字
Lü Chen	吕忱
Mei Yingzuo	梅膺祚
Mencius	孟子
Mencius, the	《孟子》
Ming dynasty	明朝
Mister *Lü's* Spring and Autumn Annals	《吕氏春秋》
monosyllabic words	单音节词
Mt. *Yi* Stele	峄山刻石
mutually explanatory characters	转注字
Newly Compiled Elementary Student Dictionary, the	《新编小学生字典》
oracle bone script	甲骨文
origin	起源
Ouyang Pucun	欧阳溥存
Peiligang culture	裴李岗文化
personal computer	个人电脑
Phoenician alphabetic script	腓利基字母文字
phonemic characters	音素文字
phonetic loan characters	假借字
pictographic characters	象形字
pictophonetic characters	形音字
pinyin	拼音
polyphones	多音字

Sumerian cuneiform	苏美尔楔形文字
syllabic characters	音节文字
syllable	音节
Tai'an	泰安
Tang dynasty	唐朝
Thousand Character Classic	《千字文》
Thousand Characters for Civilians	《平民千字课》
Three Character Classic	《三字经》
tone	音调
tone sign	音调符号
vowel	元音
Wang Xizhi	王羲之
Wang Yirong	王懿荣
Water Margin	《水浒传》
web page	网页
Wubizixing input method	五笔字型输入法
Wuyang	舞阳
WWW (World Wide Web)	万维网
Xi'an	西安
Xi'an Stele Forest	西安碑林
Xia dynasty	夏朝
***Xinhua* Dictionary**	《新华字典》
Xu Shen	许慎
Xu Zhongshu	徐中舒
Xuanmi Pagoda Stele	玄秘塔碑
Xunzi	荀子
Xunzuanpian	《训纂篇》
Yang Xiong	扬雄
Yangshao culture	仰韶文化
Yangzi River	长江
Yanshi	偃师
Yellow Emperor	皇帝
Yellow River	黄河
Yin dynasty	殷朝
Yinxu	殷墟
Yupian	《玉篇》
Zhang Qiyun	张其昀

Zhang Xu	张旭
Zhang Yushu	张玉书
Zhou dynasty	周朝
zhuyin	注音
Zihui	《字汇》
Zilin	《字林》

Index
索引